What's the Deal with®...

Reverse Mortgages?

Second Edition

SHELLEY GIORDANO, MA

Founder and Chair Funding Longevity Task Force

Praise

"Shelley's second edition has brought her book on reverse mortgages fully up-to-date, and it remains the most consumer-friendly explanation about how reverse mortgages can help improve retirement outcomes. Shelley strikes the perfect balance between explaining how reverse mortgages work in simple terms, while also fully grounding everything she says within academic research. I can't recommend her book enough for those interested to learn more about this retirement planning tool."

— **Wade Pfau, PhD, CFA**
Professor of Retirement Income,
American College of Financial Services

"What's the Deal with Reverse Mortgages? is a well-written and comprehensive resource for homeowners and financial planners who want to understand the Home Equity Conversion Mortgage (HECM). It offers a compelling roadmap to assess both time-tested and new strategies for using this type of loan to solve financial challenges and increase peace of mind in retirement."

— **Barbara R Stucki, PhD**
Consultant, BRStucki Consulting

"There is a looming retirement crisis, and one's home is going to be a critical source of retirement income support, especially among lower-income households. This was the first book I read on reverse mortgages, and I was pleased to find that each facet is examined in great detail yet is also tangible for even the novice reader. Shelley's lucid prose and extensive research on reverse mortgages makes this a must-read for individuals, investment advisors, and policymakers keen to learn more about this topic and contribute to global retirement security."

— **Arun Muralidhar, PhD**
Co-Founder, Mcube Investment Technologies

Contents

Preface To The Second Edition: Why Home Equity?   1

ONE: The Greatest Reverse Mortgage Of All Time   7

TWO: Who Created Reverse Mortgages In The US?   11

THREE: What The Press Gets Wrong: The 4 Nevers©   17
  HECM Never #1   19
  HECM Never #2   20
  HECM Never #3   20
  HECM Never #4   21
  Conclusion   23

FOUR: What Are The Differences Between The HECM
And Traditional Lending?   25
  What if?   29
  How are funds distributed in reverse mortgages?   29
  How are costs paid?   30
  Comparison of final equity versus home value   32
  Conclusion   35

FIVE: How About A HELOC Versus A HECM Line Of Credit?   37

Qualifying for a HELOC versus a HECM line of credit   39
Set-up costs for a HELOC versus a HECM line of credit   39
Protection against deteriorating market forces   40
Still confused?   45
Conclusion   46

SIX: Meeting Retirement Needs With Unusually Flexible Terms   49

Flexible feature one   50
Flexible feature two   50
Flexible feature three   51
Flexible feature four   55
Flexible feature five   56
Conclusion   56

SEVEN: What Happens At Loan's End?   57

Snowbirds   58
When a borrower enters a nursing home   58
Death or permanent departure   59
Eligible non-borrowing spouse deferral period   61
If a borrower wants to pay off the HECM but continue living in the house   64
Conclusion   64

EIGHT: Can You Really Buy A House Using A Reverse Mortgage?   67

Purchasing a new principal residence versus buying a second home   68
How HECM purchase money is calculated   70
Conclusion   75

NINE: Housing Wealth Is Not A Last-Resort Strategy 77

1. Longevity risk   78
2. 401(k): Risk for funding retirement has shifted to the individual   79
3. Market volatility: Sequence of returns risk and reverse dollar-cost averaging   81

Sequence of returns risk   82

Reverse dollar-cost averaging   87

4. Consumption and the risk of declining purchasing power   90

Barry Sacks: How a reverse mortgage protects cash flow   92

Conclusion   98

TEN: When To Draw Strategically From A Reverse Mortgage 99

Lump sum and mandatory obligations   100

Encore career   102

Term payment   102

Tenure payment: A cash flow floor like an annuity   103

Line of credit: The shock absorber   109

Combination   114

Conclusion   116

ELEVEN: What Professor Wade Pfau Discovered About Reverse Mortgages 117

Social Security bridge   121

Conclusion   122

TWELVE: Other Strategies For Using Housing Wealth In Retirement Planning 123

Divorce in silver years: Realtors©, pay close attention!   125

Tax equivalents   127

Tax bracket creep   128
Understanding how interest payments on
  HECM loans are deductible   128
Acquisition debt versus consumption
  (home equity) debt   129
When interest is paid   129
The payment waterfall for purposes of
  deducting interest   130
Tax bunching   131
The lost tax deduction for estate planning   132
Tax-free way to fund other financial needs?   133
Long-term care   133
Roth Conversion taxes and NUA   134
Defer Social Security by using the HECM as
  an income bridge   135
The HECM as a hedge against inflation   138
Medicare gap: Watch your MAGI   140
The HECM as a hedge against declining home values   141
Caution: The ruthless option   142
Home care   143
Funding for real estate taxes with the HECM LESA   146
Conclusion   148

THIRTEEN: The Cash-Poor Myth   151
No evidence for the last-resort strategy   154
Coordinated versus Uncoordinated Approach   154
Exit strategy   155
Conclusion   156

**FOURTEEN: When A Financial Adviser Will
Not/Cannot Discuss The Housing Asset   157**
Fined for helping a client with a reverse mortgage   158
The folly of wait-and-see   160

FINRA 161

Financial planning software deficiencies 162

Paying for advice 163

Ignoring cash flow in retirement advice 164

Preserving assets under management 164

Who doesn't need a backup plan for
a secure retirement? 165

How can an adviser change the
compliance prohibition? 166

Firm study group 167

Standard of care 168

Conclusion 169

**FIFTEEN: Finding An Ethical Lender And
Getting The Best Price? 171**

If the HECM will be in place for a short period of time 173

If the HECM will be used to establish a
standby line of credit 174

If the HECM is used to purchase a new
principal residence 174

If the HECM will be used to refinance an
existing traditional mortgage/HELOC 175

If the HECM will be disbursed in a term or
tenure payment schedule 175

Negotiating interest rates and fees 175

FHA counseling is mandatory before application:
How to find a counselor 180

Finding a lender 180

Filing a complaint 181

For those who already have a reverse mortgage 181

Other red flags 182

Conclusion 184

SIXTEEN: The Application Process   **187**
   The appraisal   187
   Underwriting and the life-expectancy set-aside (LESA)   188
   Processing   189
   Closing   190
   Servicing   190

SEVENTEEN: Nuts And Bolts: Typical FAQs   **191**

EIGHTEEN: Robert C. Merton, Nobel Laureate:
Reverse Mortgages Around The World   **199**
   UK   200
   Canada   201
   South Korea   202
   Japan   203
   Australia   203
   New Zealand   204
   China   205
   Singapore   206
   Italy   207
   France   207
   Spain   207
   Conclusion   208

NINETEEN: Conclusion: Do Not Wait   **209**
   The ultimate interest-only mortgage   211

Resources   **215**
Glossary   **221**
Appendix For Advanced Study   **233**
Acknowledgments   **239**
The History Of The Funding Longevity Task Force   **243**
The Author   **245**

This book is dedicated to my mentor

Barry H. Sacks, PhD, JD

and other members of the

Funding Longevity Task Force

Marguerita Cheng, CFP

Thomas C. B. Davison, MA, PhD, CFP

Wade Pfau, PhD, CFA

Sandra Timmermann, EdD

Curtis Cloke, CLTC, LUTCF, RICP

Jamie Hopkins, Esq., LLM, CFP, ChFC, CLU, RICP

Betty Meredith, CFA, CFP, CRC

Peter Neuwirth, FSA, FCA

Anna Rappaport, FSA, MAAA

Barbara Stucki, PhD

Steve Thomas, CLU, ChFC, LUTCF

Craig Lemoine, PhD, CFP

Preface To The Second Edition: Why Home Equity?

I wrote this book for advisers, their clients, and the millions of retirement DIYers who are searching for the truth about what is likely their largest asset, their home. According to the US Census Bureau, home equity represents roughly two-thirds of the average retiree's net worth.[1] Yet, this asset is largely ignored by both advisers and consumers. My goal is to bring the home asset to the forefront.

This book is a bridge between an adviser's point of view and the consumer. Although it is somewhat technical, and aimed at the financial professional, you may notice that I often address the homeowner directly when I am especially passionate about the point at hand. I tackle the topic of reverse mortgage mechanics, but I reserved it for later in the book in order to emphasize how important it is to be thinking about the home as a retirement asset early in the retirement process. In this second edition, I am focused on three concepts that warrant attention from anyone considering crafting a secure retirement:

• Reverse mortgages are not a last resort option

• As there is no labor income in retirement, it is essential to manage fixed expenses and preserve cash flow

• Having a reverse mortgage in place can absorb the inevitable spending and liquidity shocks in a long retirement

In 2015, when the first edition was published, we were just on the cusp of really understanding how the housing asset could improve retirement income security. Not knowing that, I plunged in anyway and published what was then the first compilation of research on the topic. Three years later, there is no ambiguity as to the utility of evaluating housing wealth in planning for an uncertain retirement horizon. In fact, enabling countries with dwindling birthrates to support an aging population that is living longer than ever before is one of the great public policy challenges of our time. I live in Washington, DC and am amazed at the number of think tanks, regulatory agencies, NGOs, universities, and financial services firms that are focused on how precarious retirement income security is for many Americans.

And yet most retirees own a home. It is what Robert C. Merton, Nobel Laureate in Economics, terms "an asset retirees already own; nothing has to be created." We know that retirees strongly prefer aging in the comfort and familiarity of their own homes. Over the years, homeowners have created housing wealth by systematically making monthly mortgage payments. Life-cycle theories propose that once a homeowner retires, the savings that are accumulated in the house should flow back to help support the homeowner in his or her home in retirement. Sounds logical, right?

Not so fast. Even though there are trillions of dollars in senior equity, a number that dwarfs other assets, people are still reluctant to extract some of that wealth through a reverse mortgage. Why is this asset ignored by people who could benefit from using it?

Well, first there is evidence that seniors accommodate themselves to smaller and smaller budgets quite naturally. In the US retirement system, few people have pensions coming in from their employers. They are relying on their own savings, investments, 401(k)s, and IRAs to meet their needs in retirement, along with Social Security. Basically, we are asking retirees on Day One of retirement to make the change from saver to borrower. A recent study confirmed that retirees are frugal and actually hold on to their savings for decades rather than take a chance at depleting them.[2] No doubt retirees feel just as protective of their home assets. Many hold on to them as a kind of ultimate backstop: "It will take care of me in my old age."

What we have learned from retirement income scholars, however, is that the home asset can substantially improve retirement security when used thoughtfully. No one is suggesting that seniors plunder their home equity, but there are legitimate situations where liquefying home equity can significantly reduce stress and improve peace of mind. Using a reverse mortgage to buy a new age-appropriate home, or replacing a traditional mortgage with a reverse mortgage, accomplishes two related goals that retirement income experts recommend pursuing:

- Reduce fixed expenses in retirement to help avoid drawing from savings in a down market
- Invest in your own cash flow

Without labor income and with a finite reserve of savings, the retiree is vulnerable to spending shocks of all kinds, including portfolio shock. The Home Equity Conversion Mortgage (HECM) reverse mortgage stands by to absorb whatever quakes lie in store over a twenty-to-forty-year retirement, including:

- Portfolio shock
- Liquidity shock
- Divorce shock
- Dental work
- Inflation shock
- Health shock
- Car repairs
- Hearing aids
- New roof

As you read this book, you will learn the basics of retirement income planning and how the housing asset fits into the puzzle.[3] I am not a planner and am not pretending to be one; I realize that it is the opinions of the brilliant minds living in the retirement income world that will sway your thinking about reverse mortgages. Although there is no one more passionate about changing the bad rap of reverse mortgages, I have done my best to keep my personal views muted while depending on experts and scholarship to tell the story.

Shelley Giordano
December, 2018

Notes

1 US Census Bureau, *Survey of Income and Program Participation, Wealth Tables 2011, Table 1: Median Value of Assets for Households 2011.*

2 Sudipto Banerjee, "Asset Decumulation or Asset Preservation? What Guides Retirement Spending?" EBRI Education and Research Fund, Employee Benefits Research Institute, April 3, 2018, No. 447.

3 For a discussion of what retirees will be spending their money on, see https://www.newretirement.com/retirement/the-highest-retirement-cost-that-no-one-talks-about/. You may be surprised to learn that transportation at 16% comes in behind housing (33.9%), both of which are higher than healthcare costs at 13.4%.

ONE

The Greatest Reverse Mortgage Of All Time

Jeanne Marie Calment is the oldest documented human who ever lived. Madame Calment lived in Arles, France, from February 21, 1875 to August 4, 1997. She outlived both of her daughters and her grandson by decades. Astoundingly, she lived to celebrate her 122nd birthday.

Calment funded her longevity with the world's most successful reverse mortgage.

In 1965, at the age of ninety, she entered a private agreement to sell her apartment to lawyer André-François Raffray. Raffray, then forty-seven, agreed to pay her a monthly sum of 2,500 francs until she died, at which point he would take possession of her apartment. This transaction was a rudimentary reverse mortgage. Basically,

Raffray was betting that Madame Calment would die shortly, making his monthly 2,500-franc investment a sweet deal.

What he failed to take into account was the potential for human longevity. He actually died first, in 1995 at age seventy-seven, while the formidable Madame Calment kept on living. Under the terms of this private reverse mortgage, his widow was obligated to continue the payments until Calment exited the home. The Raffray family ended up paying Calment the equivalent of more than $180,000, double the apartment's value. This reverse mortgage worked out very well for the borrower because Madame Calment beat the longevity odds, but what about the lender? Monsieur Raffray did not make out so well.

What if the circumstances had been inverted? What if Madame Calment had died a few months after "selling" her house to Monsieur Raffray? Although we do not know if Monsieur Raffray guaranteed a minimum payout, it is possible that he would have been able to buy the house for a proverbial song.

This conundrum brings us to the crux of reverse mortgage lending. With the original reverse mortgages, both the lender and the borrower were at risk depending on whether the borrower's lifespan was either short or long. The borrower's short lifespan would favor the lender; a long lifespan subjects the lender to potential loss, just like Monsieur Raffray. Likewise, a short lifespan would subject the borrower's estate to potential loss if very little cash is disbursed before death. No one would want to enter a reverse mortgage transaction if the lender takes the title without regard for the amount of money actually advanced to the borrower.

So how can both the borrower and the lender be protected? Enter the United States Congress.

TWO

Who Created Reverse Mortgages In The US?

Some people have heard that a reverse mortgage is a scheme or a scam perpetrated on helpless seniors. Others may consider a reverse mortgage a welfare handout. Many are surprised to learn that the 100th US Congress initiated the modern reverse mortgage with the 1987 Housing and Community Development Act, and that it was signed by President Ronald Reagan in February 1988.

The US Congress tasked the Federal Housing Authority (FHA) with designing a reverse mortgage that protected the elderly but would encourage lending in the private sector as well. In December of 1988, the Department of Housing and Urban Development (HUD) published a notice asking potential mortgage lenders to participate in a demonstration program that "will insure up to 2,500 reverse mortgages on the homes of elderly homeowners, enabling them to turn their equity into cash." Under the HECM Insurance Demonstration, the modern reverse mortgage was born.

In this way, the FHA solved the problem of protecting both the homeowner and the lender. It modified the existing FHA insurance program to fit reverse lending. Understanding how the FHA operates in traditional lending provides a helpful comparison. Created in 1934, as part of the National Housing Act, the FHA provides mortgage insurance on loans made by FHA-approved lenders throughout the United States and its territories. The FHA insures mortgages on single-family and multi-family homes, including manufactured homes and hospitals. It is the largest insurer of mortgages in the world, insuring over 34 million properties since its inception. In 1965 the FHA became a part of HUD.

At the height of the Depression, Congress and President Franklin Roosevelt created an incentive for lenders to provide financing for certain higher-risk borrowers by protecting the lenders from loss. FHA insurance premiums were assessed on these loans and provided the funds to insure against loss. In traditional FHA loans, homeowners pay upfront and monthly insurance premiums that provide lenders with protection against losses should the homeowner default. The FHA lenders bear less risk because the FHA will pay a claim to the lender in the event of a homeowner's default. To qualify for insurance protection these loans must meet specific requirements established by the FHA.[1]

As we know, insurance is predicated on the participation of the many to cover the losses of the few. *In other words, the participants pool funds (via paying premiums). These funds in turn transfer risk to the insurance entity.* Ingeniously, the new reverse mortgage, the HECM, adopted the FHA insurance concept, but tinkered with it in the following ways in order to adapt to reverse mortgage needs:

1. Insurance premiums are not paid monthly but are added to the loan balance.

2. The homeowner/estate is released from liability should the loan balance exceed the home value.

3. If the home value does not cover the loan balance, the lender is protected by the FHA.

As you can see, the FHA solved the problem. The resulting HECM, which includes FHA insurance, is designed to encourage lenders to finance cash disbursals, but should circumstances not go as anticipated, the lenders cannot lose on the money they have financed. Additionally, the HECM protects the homeowner (and his or her estate) from loss should the homeowner live so long that the loan balance grows beyond the home value. The consumer safeguards are substantial and are becoming progressively better both for the individual borrower *and* the tax payer.

Unfortunately, these HECM consumer safeguards seem to elude the financial press, and many of the financial advisers on whom many Americans rely for accurate information on their retirement options.

Even with HUD's continued efforts to refine the program, over time program weaknesses emerged. Especially during the housing bubble years, the HECM was used to bail out hopeless situations. Some people took reverse mortgages but did not take seriously the requirement that they keep up to date on tax and insurance obligations. In other cases, a number of younger spouses not on title were displaced when the borrower died. And finally, some borrowers used the HECM irresponsibly by drawing down their entire initial credit limits at closing, leaving no cushion for falling home values. These were serious problems and jeopardized the program and its reputation. In response, the 113th Congress passed the Reverse Mortgage Stabilization Act of 2013. It was enacted in order to protect not only the non-borrowing spouses but to restore financial health to the FHA Mutual Mortgage Insurance Fund. Over the years, the HECM program has been self-sustaining; the insurance pool was never intended to be a taxpayer bail-out. When the housing bubble collapsed, however, the fund's solvency was in jeopardy. HUD responded by changing lending standards, and the HECM, in particular, was altered significantly. As a result, the fund's economic strength is improving.[2]

Financial assessments are now a basis for HECM loan approval. To counteract the effects of potential tax and insurance defaults, there are formulas to set aside equity to assure that tax and insurance costs are paid. These set-asides are required for those who cannot establish willingness and capacity to meet these basic housing obligations. To bolster program safety, limits have been placed on how much equity can be drawn early in the loan. Finally, a non-borrowing spouse (NBS) status was created to allow a younger spouse not old enough to borrow (sixty-two years old is the minimum borrowing age) to remain in the home if the actual borrower dies.

So rather than being a fraudulent scheme designed to fleece seniors, the modern reverse mortgage, aka the HECM, is a program put in place by the government of the United States. As FHA Commissioner Brian Montgomery is fond of saying, the HECM is the "law of the land." Admittedly the HECM was not perfect at inception. But like many financial products, the program has evolved. HUD continues to fine-tune the program to provide better consumer safety as well as improved risk management for the insurance pool.

A reverse mortgage is neither bad nor good in and of itself. Its value lies in how the borrower uses it.

Notes

1   These requirements are listed on the HUD website: http://portal.hud.gov/hudportal/HUD?src=/program_offices/ housing/fhahistory.

2   www.reversereview.com/nrmla-news/nrmla-news-25.html.

THREE

What The Press Gets Wrong: The 4 Nevers©

Early on in HECM history, potential borrowers had a very difficult time finding information on reverse mortgages. Few banks provided the product, the internet was not accessible for many, and the television commercials advertising and describing the product had not begun.

I will always remember the first call I took from a bewildered and timid customer. Mrs. Burns was salt-of-the-earth, had paid every bill on time for her entire life, and was absolutely mortified to be making a call to a mortgage company confessing her need for information on reverse mortgages. When we got to talking, her story was heartbreaking. Her husband had bladder cancer, and although the doctors were finding ways to keep him alive, their insurance was woefully inadequate. Her bills for his medical and nutritional care had mounted to the point that she was borrowing from one credit card to pay another. Her husband, understandably, had pretty much checked out as he coped with his cancer. This left her alone and frightened. I still remember her telling me that she could not take her grandchildren out for ice cream cones. Having no other resources for information, her only choice was to call a stranger. She really did not even know what questions to ask. Although we were able to help her, and even had a credit card cutting ceremony at the closing, we wanted to find an easy way, a kind of checklist, for clients so that their unconscious fears of the Reverse Mortgage Boogie Man were both uncovered and addressed when they called.

Over time we developed the 4 Nevers list. This simple list proved to be extremely useful in helping clients confirm what they thought they knew about reverse mortgages. Even more, the list helped clients stand up to well-meaning but misinformed friends, ministers, children, and even hairdressers who were giving them advice on whether or not to pursue a reverse mortgage.

So here it is. If you memorize the 4 Nevers, you can have a conversation with anyone on reverse mortgages and defend your understanding against those who opine on reverse mortgages *often without the least bit of factual knowledge*. The fact is the HECM always has provided essential safeguards for the consumer from the beginning, even before the most recent legislation. So even if it is wise to avoid using the word "never" in life, homeowner fears are allayed via an understanding of the HECM 4 Nevers:[1]

HECM Never #1

Remember Madame Calment? When she entered the reverse mortgage with Monsieur Raffray, she relinquished ownership of her home. It worked out well for her, but no homeowner wants to give up control of the home. With the HECM, home ownership remains with the borrower. In other words: The bank does not ever get the house.

The HECM is a mortgage like any other but with deferred payment. When the homeowner leaves the house, there is a mortgage attached to the home that must be paid. The homeowner's heirs can elect to pay off the HECM (but never have to pay more than 95% of the home value) by acquiring their own financing, thereby keeping the house in the family.

Alternatively, they can elect to sell the house with any remaining profit being theirs to keep. The HECM, unlike some older reverse mortgages, does not allow the lender to take an equity share on appreciated value. All available equity beyond the loan balance belongs to the borrower or the estate. Additionally, if the loan is underwater, they may grant the lender a deed-in-lieu, hand over the keys, and literally walk away. The lender's loss is made good by the FHA insurance pool, with no recourse to the borrower or the estate.

Remember, foreclosure can happen when taxes, insurance, and reasonable home maintenance are not provided by the homeowner. Taxes, insurance, and home maintenance (including HOA fees) are the only mandatory funding obligations for the borrower.

HECM Never #2

The HECM protects the borrower and all heirs. The loan documents state that "no deficiency judgment may be taken against the borrower or his estate." It is not possible for the parents to leave a reverse mortgage debt to their children to have to pay.

This safeguard is possible because the HECM is a non-recourse loan. When a person applies for the HECM, the borrower is not required to verify that the loan can be repaid. The house alone serves as collateral for the loan. If the estate sells the house to satisfy the HECM loan balance, any remaining equity belongs to the heirs. The lender cannot access any equity beyond the loan balance. The heirs may retire the mortgage for 95% of the home's appraised value, or the loan amount, whichever is less.

HECM Never #3

Some people think that people with reverse mortgages have given their homes to the bank, and once the bank decides it has lent enough money, it can throw the home-owners to the curb and force them to move. We have already seen that the HECM protects ownership and that the borrower never gives up the title, just like any mortgage. Yet unlike other mortgages, the HECM does not have a "maturity" or required end date.

Well, technically there is an end date, but one that should not give much worry. The HECM comes due on the 150th birthday of the youngest borrower, but even Madame Calment did not get close to that. The loan does require meeting obligations of home ownership, *just as any mortgage does*. The homeowner must maintain his or her property taxes, *just like any mortgage*. The homeowner must maintain property insurance to protect against fire and other hazards, *just like any mortgage*. Additionally, the borrower must not allow the home to fall to ruin, *just like any mortgage*.

So let's bring up that ugly word: Foreclosure. In the go-go years of easy credit and rapidly increasing home appreciation, some borrowers used a reverse mortgage like an ATM. They stripped their home equity and could not, or would not, pay their tax and insurance obligations. Under the terms of the loan, lenders were faced with foreclosing in these cases.

Foreclosing on seniors is tragic under any circumstances and reporters had a heyday with it. The fact is these technical foreclosures had nothing to do with the loan being a reverse mortgage. Tax and insurance default can result in foreclosure for mortgages, period. There is nothing special about a reverse mortgage in this regard.

HECM Never #4

However, there is something special about reverse mortgages and foreclosure beyond taxes and insurance. The risk of foreclosure with a HECM is fundamentally and drastically different. This is because monthly payments are never required. Therefore, no foreclosure based on non-payment can ever happen.

So think about this: is Homeowner #1, who carries a traditional mortgage requiring monthly debt service, better off than Homeowner #2, who cannot lose the home by missing payments? At minimum you must admit that there is greater risk of foreclosure for anyone holding a standard amortizing loan (with payments) versus a reverse mortgage (with no payments required). As long as taxes, insurance, and maintenance obligations are met, the HECM persists until the last borrower, or eligible non-borrowing spouse, dies, moves, or sells.

The HECM loan documents state this feature in unambiguous terms:

> No deficiency judgments. Borrower shall have no personal liability for payment of the debt secured by this Security Instrument. Lender may enforce the debt only through sale of the Property. Lender shall not be permitted to obtain a deficiency judgment against Borrower if the Security Instrument is foreclosed. If this Security Instrument is assigned to the Secretary upon demand by the Secretary, Borrower shall not be liable for any difference between the mortgage insurance benefits paid to Lender and the outstanding indebtedness, including accrued interest, owed by Borrower at the time of the assignment.

In other words, the lender can assign the loan to FHA ("the Secretary" of HUD) to recoup losses and the borrower has no personal responsibility for the loan. Regardless of what the loan balance becomes, as long as home ownership obligations are met, the HECM is totally open-ended. The home is there to serve the borrower for as long as he or she lives in the house, all thanks to FHA insurance.

Conclusion

The FHA Home Equity Conversion Mortgage remains the gold standard in reverse mortgage lending. Over the years, proprietary reverse mortgages with similar consumer safeguards have been marketed, but the HECM continues to provide the highest loan to value, lowest rates, and most flexibility. But because the FHA lending limit is capped today at $726,525, homeowners with high mortgage balances will want to explore products not insured by FHA, known in the mortgage business as Jumbo reverse mortgages. And for those with very expensive homes, the private Jumbo reverse mortgage may provide quite a bit more cash.

Notes

1   © 2000, The 4 Nevers, Shelley Giordano.

FOUR

What Are The Differences Between The HECM And Traditional Lending?

The Consumer Federal Protection Bureau (CFPB) found that some consumers do not understand from watching commercials that interest is compounding, or that proceeds from the reverse mortgage are debt, not income.[1] Yet by definition, a reverse mortgage is a negatively amortizing loan. That means that the loan balance grows from month to month because interest payments are deferred. Interest not paid is added to the amount due. The following month's interest is calculated on the new, higher loan balance. Over time, the HECM loan balance can grow quickly.

Amortize literally means "kill the debt." In a traditional loan, periodic monthly payments reduce the debt over time. Payments are applied to the interest and a small amount to the principal. Over time, the principal does decline, but the cumulative payments can easily be two to three times the original principal amount. Everyone knows that a thirty-year mortgage entails an enormous amount of interest. Of course, it is the interest payment that reimburses the lender for carrying the debt all those years.

In a traditional mortgage, the homeowner is eligible to borrow an amount based on the home value, the homeowner's credit history, interest rates, and the required down payment. The more skin in the game a homeowner provides in a down payment, the more favorable the loan terms may be.

In reverse mortgage lending, the credit available at the outset of the loan is generally less. A borrower must be at least sixty-two years old and have obtained a counseling certificate from an FHA-approved counselor. The property is subject to FHA lending codes and must either pass an FHA appraisal or be brought to standards before or soon after closing.

Although a HECM is not required to negatively amortize, it is assumed that the loan will have a growing loan balance. A homeowner always may elect to keep the loan balance low by making voluntary payments to offset interest accrual. Usually, though, homeowners do not reduce debt because they decide against making any payments on both the interest and principal. To accommodate that growing debt, there must be a cushion of equity to pay the loan back. The HECM initial credit limit, therefore, is determined in part by age and prevailing interest rates.

26

That cushion for accumulating interest makes the HECM what Melissa and Pilar Patterson-Kling of Reverse Engineer Lab term a "self-financing loan."

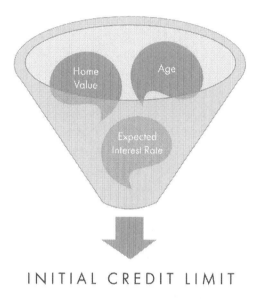

INITIAL CREDIT LIMIT

Figure 4.1: *FHA Calculation for determining how much equity can be accessed at loan's inception*

Because the FHA insures the loan, a HECM is subject to the FHA lending limit, which is $726,525. A house can be worth more than $726,525, of course, and still qualify for a reverse mortgage, but values beyond the lending limit are invisible for purposes of calculating available credit. For example, if the house appraises for $800,000, the borrower will be eligible for the same amount of cash as if the house had appraised for $726,525. There will just be more equity cushion beyond the loan amount.

The age of the youngest participant and the expected interest rate determine the Principal Limit factor. This factor adjusts the initial maximum borrowing limit based on actuarial assumptions and what the interest rate over the course of the loan may be. Think of the Principal Limit as a loan to value (LTV) that grows every month because the loan balance is growing. HUD frequently alters the Principal Limit factors and sometimes the lending limit in order to manage program risk.

Principal Limit factors are published by the Secretary of HUD and are based on the following underlying concepts, subject to the overall FHA lending limit:

- **The greater the home value** the greater the amount that can be borrowed

- **The older the borrower** the greater the amount that can be borrowed

- **The lower the interest rate** the greater the amount that can be borrowed

Table 4.1: *Comparison of initial borrowing limit by age for $400,000 home value (may vary by lender)*

Homeowner's Age (Youngest)	Home Value $400,000	Mortgage Balance $400,000	Estimated Initial Cash Available
62	$400,000	$0	$140,600
82	$400,000	$0	$200,600

Calculations are from www.rfslends.com/tools on August 6, 2018. These calculations assume that there is no mortgage on the property. These calculations are for illustration only.

What if?

What if the FHA assumptions fail on any given loan? Say rising interest rates cause the loan balance to outstrip the home value? What if the client lives to 122? What if housing values drop? That's what the FHA mortgage insurance pool is for: protection for both the lender and the borrower. The borrower is insulated from any loss. The lender's loss is covered by FHA insurance.

How are funds distributed in reverse mortgages?

Although these features will be discussed later, it is helpful to understand that reverse mortgage draws are flexible throughout the life of the loan, particularly when the adjustable-rate mortgage is chosen and provided the credit limit has not been exhausted. It is possible to lock in a fixed interest rate with a HECM, but the adjustable rate is far more flexible. With a HECM line of credit, homeowners could be borrowing at a distant time in the future, so the lender will want to make sure that the future rates they are charged are close to their cost of money at the time the homeowners draw on the line. Because the lender is protected with a variable rate, the initial cost of an adjustable rate is usually lower than a fixed rate. The options for drawing on the adjustable-rate HECM are:

- **Lump sum:** A draw on funds up to the current credit limit

- **Tenure payment:** A guaranteed monthly payment as long as the last borrower lives in the house

- **Term payment:** A monthly payment for a predetermined term

- **Line of credit:** Credit held in reserve, but growing in capacity monthly

- **Combination:** A combination of any of the above

Although the house does not need to be free of mortgages, whatever liens exist must be paid off either by the homeowner or through the proceeds available at the loan's outset.

How are costs paid?

Because actuarial tables and prevailing interest rates determine how much a homeowner can borrow at the outset of the loan, repayment can be deferred until the last borrower dies, moves, or sells. Typical mortgage closing costs, lender fees, are rolled into the loan, but there is one big difference between FHA loans and those not insured. Insurance of any kind has a cost, and the HECM is no different. There is an initial FHA mortgage insurance premium (MIP) that is rolled into the loan as well, and this becomes part of the loan balance. As the mortgage progresses, any draws, ongoing MIP, and loan costs are added to the loan balance. At the loan's end, either the borrower or the estate retains ownership and has to decide how to pay back the loan balance. This is done by selling the house (and keeping the remaining equity) or by retaining the house by arranging new financing. If the house is underwater, neither the borrower nor the estate has an obligation to make good on the loan. In this situation, the estate may retire the loan for 95% of appraised value regardless of the loan amount outstanding.

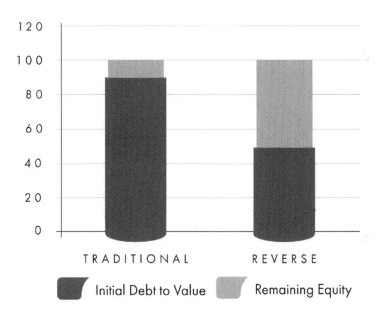

Figure 4.2: *Comparison of initial credit limit versus home value*

In the chart above, notice how a traditional mortgage would compare to a reverse mortgage. In this example, the homeowner qualifies to borrow 90% of the home's value. The upper segment represents the 10% down payment made on the house. The homeowner will make payments to pay off the debt for twenty to thirty years. Thus, the lower segment will diminish (and the upper segment will increase) during that period. On a $400,000 initial loan amount at 5% interest, this borrower would pay **$373,000** in interest over thirty years, making the total payback $773,000.

As we have seen, the HECM credit limit is determined by the borrower's age when the loan is initiated. The older the homeowner, the more money can be borrowed. Actuarial tables predict that any given older person will generally exit the home sooner than a younger person. And because the house pays the loan back, younger people will have lower initial access to funds than older people.

Comparison of final equity versus home value

In this example, the homeowner is around seventy years old and qualifies for a reverse mortgage loan equal to 50% of the home value. Because the loan balance will be going up during the ensuing years (unless voluntary payments are made), the amount that can be borrowed is limited, as the homeowner can be expected to live in the home many more years. The upper segment here represents the cushion to accommodate the rising debt. Thus, during the period in which the borrower remains in the house, the lower segment (debt) will increase, and the upper segment (equity) will diminish.

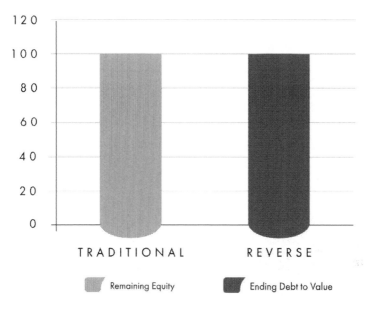

Remaining Equity   Ending Debt to Value

Figure 4.3: *Comparison of equity percentage at end of loan—traditional versus reverse (with no payments)*

The chart above compares a traditional mortgage with a reverse mortgage at the end of the loan. The traditional loan has been completely paid off, although the homeowner has paid out two to three times the home value to the lender in interest and principal. The time value burden is significant in traditional lending when considering the loss of cash flow over many years. As my colleague Jim Spicka observed, "The money you have in your pocket today is slowly buying back your equity via monthly payments." In contrast, the reverse debt will keep growing and equity shrinking until the last borrower dies, moves, or sells, unless the homeowner has elected to make payments. In this example, no payments were made during the loan term and therefore the reverse debt reduced the remaining equity month after month. But remember there has been zero reduction in cash flow because no payments were made. In fact, the borrowers lived so long that the loan balance is higher than the home's value. The loan is underwater.

Again, the HECM is unique with regard to how an underwater situation is resolved. To quote my colleague Jim Spicka again:

> Only the HECM allows the possibility of not having to pay back all the money you might someday owe. The FHA mortgage insurance guarantees that no matter what you actually owe, you only have to repay what you get net from the sale of the property regardless of the amount actually owing on your mortgage. This is not possible with a forward mortgage without risking default and foreclosure.

In the following example, however, the borrower's heirs have decided to refinance the house and keep it in the family. The heirs are obligated to pay either the loan balance or 95% of the home's value, whichever is less. In other words, they retain 5% of the home's value, even if their parents had lived so long in the house that their loan balance now exceeds the value of the house. In this underwater scenario, the lender will be made whole by the FHA. Both sides of the transaction have been protected.

Remember: If the heirs decide to sell the house, and the loan is not underwater, they are entitled to whatever dollars the house brings beyond the actual HECM loan balance.

Table 4.2: *Features of a HECM versus traditional lending*

	HECM Reverse	Traditional
Debt to Value (LTV) Rises	Yes	No
Monthly Payments	Voluntary	Required and can add up to 2–3X original amount borrowed over the life of the loan
Foreclosure	Not for missing payments	Yes, if principal or interest payments are not met

Conclusion

Although many aspects of a HECM resemble those of any mortgage, the differences are significant. Often homeowners are surprised that they initially do not qualify for as large a percentage of the home value as they would with a traditional mortgage. At current interest rates, a rule of thumb for borrowers in their seventies is about 50%.

The HECM program is designed to allow the home itself to pay the loan back, not the homeowner, so there must be a cushion of equity. The remaining equity serves as a reserve to accommodate a rising loan balance. Any amount of the cushion remaining at the end of the loan remains in the hands of the owner or the estate.

Note

1 www.consumerfinance.gov/blog/consumer-advisory-dont-be-misled-by-reverse-mortgage-advertising.

FIVE

How About A HELOC Versus A HECM Line Of Credit?

Many homeowners contact their banks in order to initiate a HELOC (home equity line of credit). They want a standby emergency fund just in case they need cash quickly for unexpected expenses. Some set up this liquid fund and never even draw from the credit line. It's just there for peace of mind. If HELOC borrowers do not take draws, they don't make monthly repayments to the bank. But once they draw on this credit line, monthly payments begin.

In addition, borrowers must prove to the bank that they personally can repay the HELOC loan. Some retirees are shocked to find that qualifying can be difficult because retirees usually have no regular income. The bank will look at an individual's income, assets, and credit score. Without income from a job, many retirees just cannot qualify for a HELOC, or for a mortgage of any kind. Ben Bernanke, former Chairman of the Federal Reserve, brought this issue into focus when he confessed that he had been turned down himself for a refinance of his mortgage once he left the Fed.

Like the HELOC, the HECM line of credit can serve as a standby emergency fund. Significant changes were made to the program in September 2013, and again in 2017. HUD acted to improve safeguards for borrowers and reduce the likelihood of rapid equity depletion. Information published before October 2, 2017, will not reflect these important HUD changes.

To discourage equity-stripping, the new HECM prohibits full draws on available equity for the first year, except for defined mandatory obligations. In doing so, the FHA has established an initial disbursement level for calculating initial insurance costs. Those who leave approximately 40% or more of their total credit amount in a line of credit until at least Day 366 are now assessed a 2% MIP on home value. This is an increase in upfront MIP but assures that each HECM loan is contributing appropriately to the insurance fund. In contrast, borrowers who leave less than 40% of their total initial credit limit in the line of credit before Day 366 will be charged less, a reduction from 2.5% of home value to 2.0%. As with a HELOC, interest is not charged against the HECM line until money is actually drawn. This, however, is where the similarity ends.

Qualifying for a HELOC versus a HECM line of credit

Again, to qualify, there must be one borrower at least sixty-two years old with a property insurable by FHA lending standards. FHA regulations have changed, and borrowers now are required to demonstrate willingness and ability to meet tax, insurance, and maintenance obligations. These new underwriting requirements will not rely on credit scores or be as stringent as traditional lending. This is because the property alone pays the loan back, not the individual. Going forward, however, the HECM will be available only to those who can demonstrate financial wherewithal to satisfy homeowner obligations for tax, insurance, and maintenance. These changes help ensure that the loan is appropriate for the homeowner over the long run.

Set-up costs for a HELOC versus a HECM line of credit

Today, a HECM line of credit costs more to set up than a HELOC because the loan must be insured to protect the borrower for liability for a loan balance that exceeds the home value. These costs can be mitigated if the homeowner will take the time to contact at least three lenders for a competitive bid. Be sure to balance the upfront costs with the interest rate margin as well as what origination fee, if any, is charged.

Protection against deteriorating market forces

People are surprised by yet another aspect of HECM lending. No matter what the economy does, no matter if housing values drop in the neighborhood, no matter what happens to the lender in the future, the HECM line of credit cannot be canceled, frozen, or reduced.

Table 5.1: Comparison of HECM line of credit and HELOC

Loan Terms	HECM Line of Credit	HELOC
Lender can cancel, freeze, or reduce Line of Credit	No	Yes
Monthly payment required	No	Yes
Deficiency judgment possible	No	Yes
Minimum credit score needed	No, but must demonstrate ability to meet homeowner obligations	Yes
Interest-only term expires and principal payments must commence	No	Yes
Line of Credit remains in place regardless of home value in the future	Yes	Probably not
Unused Line of Credit grows every month	Yes	No

Many financial planners remember the fate of standby HELOCs their clients had in place for a rainy day when the Great Recession hit. Just when their clients needed ready cash, the banks canceled, reduced, or froze their lines of credit. In contrast, clients who had an FHA-insured HECM line of credit were insulated from this liquidity shock because the lender cannot alter the obligation to lend. If there are remaining funds in the HECM line of credit the lender must make them available to the homeowner.[1]

As we have learned, the credit capacity in HECM lending is known as the Principal Limit. Because the typical HECM loan balance is growing every month, negatively amortizing, the credit capacity increases every month. The available credit *not* yet drawn is the HECM line of credit. And that HECM line of credit increases every month at the same rate as the Principal Limit.

The fact that the HECM line of credit increases every month is unique to the HECM. Borrowers and advisers alike are surprised, and even a bit bewildered, when they learn of this feature, because there is no other financial product that provides a guaranteed growth like this.

Figure 5.1: *Relationship of Principal Limit to loan balance and line of credit (simplified)*

The Ongoing Principal Limit is the sum of the outstanding loan balance plus a line of credit. The Principal Limit, the loan balance, and the available line of credit are all increasing at the monthly interest rate + MIP.[2]

The Principal Limit is the driver

Let's step back a minute and consider the Principal Limit. Basically, it is the amount of money the bank can lend you based on your age and current interest rates. Since the house is paying back the loan, not you, actuarial assumptions apply to how much you can borrow. The older you are, the more money can be advanced. This is because chances are high that you will be borrowing money for a shorter period of time if you start later in life. Money paid out to you increases the loan balance, as does the interest accruing on what you draw. At any point in time, the total amount of credit allowed is the Principal Limit.

So the money you are allowed to borrow grows every month. As long as the loan balance does not equal the Principal Limit, there is money available to you in a line of credit. This line of credit, being a subset of the Principal Limit, grows along with the Principal Limit.

Regardless of whether or not a client starts borrowing early, or just waits to access the line of credit, the same borrowing power will be available, or credit capacity at any given period of time, no matter what the draw pattern is. Because lenders usually do not charge servicing fees, the Principal (credit) Limit minus loan balance equals the line of credit.

Remember, the line-of-credit feature is not available in a fixed-rate HECM. It is difficult for any lender to provide funds for the future at a fixed rate. The lender just does not know what the cost of its money will be in future. Most lines of credit, reverse or traditional, adjust to a particular index. With a variable rate, the lender has hedged the possible increase in interest rates should the borrower draw on the line years later during the life of the loan.

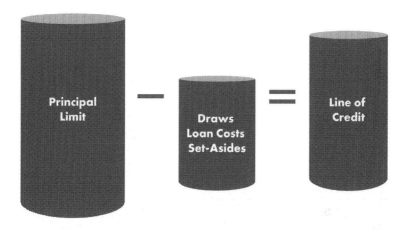

Figure 5.2: Components of Principal Limit for HECM adjustable rate

The available LOC in adjustable-rate HECMs will be the difference between the Principal Limit, draws, loan costs, and set-asides.

Table 5.2: *HECM lump sum draw versus line of credit availability/Day 366*

	HECM Withdrawal	Initial Loan Balance	Line of Credit
Client A	Takes all the available equity in a lump sum at the closing	Closing Costs Origination Fee to Lender Upfront MIP (2.0%)	**$0.** The loan balance is growing at the interest rate +.50 MIP. There is no growth in the line of credit.
Client B Same Age Same Home Value Same Interest Rate Same Closing Costs Same Origination Fee	Leaves all remaining equity in the line of credit	Closing Costs Origination Fee to Lender Upfront MIP (2.0%)	**$$$$.** The line of credit is growing at the interest rate +.50 MIP. The loan balance is growing at the exact same rate.

This table shows homeowners making two different choices about how to use the home equity in a reverse mortgage. One homeowner selects the lump sum option. The other borrows only enough on Day One to cover the costs of setting up the mortgage but leaves the rest in the line of credit.

Client A elects to take a full draw at closing (subject to eligibility). The upfront MIP is 2.0% of home value (up to $726,525). The loan balance will grow monthly at the interest rate plus one-twelfth the ongoing MIP of 50% of the loan balance. Client A does not have money left for future draws on the line of credit. Client B, of exactly the same age, home value, and interest rate, elects to leave the equity in the line of credit and retains access to the same overall credit because the line is growing at the same rate as Client A's loan balance. See how clever the HECM is:

Client B did not take a lump sum at closing but does not lose borrowing power because *the credit opportunity grows with the increasing line of credit.*

Still confused?

Okay, admittedly the growing line of credit is not the most intuitive financial concept. So, think of it this way. Let's say you take out an ABC Department Store credit card and your initial limit is $1,000. After a couple of years of being a good customer who both spends and pays back your balance in a timely manner, ABC informs you that your credit limit has increased to $1,500. This is an arbitrary increase in credit based on your borrowing relationship with ABC. You did not get an extra $500 as a gift, and if you had, you would owe taxes on it. What you got was an invitation from the lender (ABC) to use more debt at their stores. The HECM line of credit is the same, except that there is nothing arbitrary about the increase. The lender enters into a contract with you that requires the lender to make increases in your credit capacity based on a set formula. And that increase happens month over month and may not be canceled, frozen, or reduced—which of course is something ABC could do at any time.

Conclusion

Many advisers and retirees recognize the wisdom of establishing an emergency fund to meet possible needs in retirement. The cost of setting up a HECM purely as a standby will be more than that of a HELOC. A retiree would do well, however, to compare a HECM to a HELOC before deciding which standby fund makes the most sense. The set-up costs are different, as we have seen, but the stability and flexibility provided by the HECM is worth evaluating. Furthermore, the guaranteed growth in the HECM line of credit is both unique and powerful for the homeowner trying to anticipate unknowable future conditions. Because the future value of the home could be depressed at a critical time in the future, having a growing HECM line of credit in place provides protection against dropping home values. In addition, past experiences have taught us that in bad economic times when access to cash is likely needed the most, banks are under stress and are thus not a reliable source of cash flow, especially for retirees. And finally, the compulsory monthly payments start immediately for a HELOC. This constraint on cash flow in difficult times can be completely avoided with the HECM line of credit.

Notes

1   The HECM line of credit, if an adjustable rate is selected, must grow in borrowing power at a guaranteed percentage determined at closing. As long as the credit line is not exhausted, the lender is contractually obligated to make available more credit every single month at the same rate the loan balance is growing. Technically, the growth in borrowing power increases every month at the applicable monthly interest rate plus one-twelfth of the yearly MIP, if there are no set-asides in place.

2   If the loan servicer assesses servicing fees and/or set-asides, the formula could be different. In some cases, in low-interest-rate environments, the line of credit actually could decrease in a given month. Even though the credit line may shrink, the overall credit capacity has not diminished. Rather, a portion of the equity is reserved for set-asides. For a discussion of the circumstances under which an LOC could shrink, see http://reversemortgagedaily.com/2009/06/02/negative-loan-growth-hits-reverse-mortgage-credit-lines/.

SIX

Meeting Retirement Needs With Unusually Flexible Terms

We have seen how a HECM line of credit compares to a bank HELOC. Because no payments are ever required or expected, but are accepted, the borrower can choose from an array of payment methods:

- Pay the loan balance (prepayment) with no prepayment penalty

- Make payments on the interest and/or MIP and none on the principal

- Make voluntary payments any time it is convenient

- Borrower/Heir makes a balloon payment when the last borrower dies, moves, or sells

- Use the home itself to pay back the loan and have no responsibility for any sums underwater

Flexible feature one

A prepayment penalty can never be assessed against a homeowner who decides to change the decision about the reverse mortgage. If, for example, a couple initiates a reverse mortgage and then wins the lottery the next month, the loan balance can be paid in full and extinguished without penalty. Scenarios like this happen, for example, when borrowers decide to move closer to their children. The title remains with the borrower, who maintains full control over the property. There is no extra cost in paying off earlier than expected. Note that a prepayment amount in excess of the outstanding balance is not allowed. In other words, you cannot pile on to the line of credit beyond what the underlying loan to value, known as the Principal Limit, has become. In other words, the line of credit is a potential debt instrument and not a savings account.

Flexible feature two

Payments may be made against the loan balance in any amount selected by the homeowner. This feature has solved a problem for the thousands of people who borrowed via interest-only (I-O) loans during the housing bubble. These loans usually allowed a term of ten years during which a payment against the principal was not required. In fact, from 2004 to 2006, somewhere around $258 billion worth of I-O mortgages were written.

Most people understood that when the ten-year period was up, they would face an increased monthly payment, as the loan would be recast in order to start chipping away at the principal. What a lot of people did not realize was that the remaining principal amortization would be compressed. All of the principal had to be paid back in a shorter period of time; hence, people saw their monthly payments double or even triple—quite a payment shock.

Replacing a recasting I-O loan with a HECM may provide payment relief, but what if the homeowners are still working and are comfortable making a payment, just not the huge catch-up that the recast with all the unpaid principal requires? The HECM provides the flexibility to do just that. Voluntary payments are allowed but never expected or required.

Flexible feature three

In a different example, a sixty-two-year-old couple was still working and had a substantial mortgage. Their financial planner noticed that making payments was normally okay, but if they encountered unexpected expenses in retirement, those obligatory payments would compromise their savings. The planner also identified that in order to plan for longevity they should defer Social Security so that they could optimize that benefit. The couple was making monthly payments of $930 at 4% on a loan of roughly $195,000. What would happen if they replaced their mortgage with a HECM and continued making payments until they were seventy years old? (The following figures are courtesy of Keith Turner, a reverse mortgage expert in Columbus, Ohio and Thomas C. B. Davison, PhD, CFP.) And having built up their HECM line of credit, could they supplement their Social Security at age seventy once they stopped working?

In this example, the borrower replaced a mortgage with a HECM reverse mortgage and continued to make voluntary payments of $930 each month ($11,160 per year) for eight years to supplement his income while delaying Social Security benefits. In doing so, he built up his line of credit from $11,435 to $110,892. Notice his remaining home equity is back up to $471,104.

Table 6.1: Making voluntary payments of $930 during Social Security deferral 62–70

Year	Age	Payments		Interest rate	End of Year Projection				
		To You	By You		Loan Balance (with MIP)	Line Of Credit	Property Value	Equity	Principal Limit
Initial	62	$0	$11,160	4.800%	212,000	0	500,000	287,575	212,000
1	62	0	11,160	4.800%	212,078	11,435	520,000	307,497	223,513
2	63	0	11,160	4.800%	212,160	23,491	540,800	328,215	235,651
3	64	0	11,160	4.800%	212,247	36,202	562,432	349,760	248,449
4	65	0	11,160	4.800%	212,338	49,603	584,929	372,166	261,941
5	66	0	11,160	4.800%	212,434	63,732	608,326	395,467	276,166
6	67	0	11,160	4.800%	212,535	78,628	632,660	419,699	291,164
7	68	0	11,160	4.800%	212,642	94,334	657,966	444,898	306,976
8	69	0	11,160	4.800%	212,755	110,892	684,285	471,104	323,647
9	70	0	0	4.800%	224,309	116,914	711,656	486,922	341,223
10	71	0	0	4.800%	236,491	123,263	740,122	503,206	359,754

In this comparison, the borrower elected to replace his mortgage with a HECM reverse mortgage in order to reduce his expenses while deferring Social Security but did not choose to make voluntary payments.

Table 6.2: Replace mortgage with HECM without making payments

Year	Age	Payments To You	Payments By You	Interest rate	Loan Balance (with MIP)	Line Of Credit	Property Value	Equity	Principal Limit
Initial	62	$0	$0	4.800%	212,000	0	500,000	287,575	212,000
1	62	0	0	4.800%	223,513	0	520,000	296,062	223,513
2	63	0	0	4.800%	235,651	0	540,800	304,724	235,651
3	64	0	0	4.800%	248,449	0	562,432	313,558	248,449
4	65	0	0	4.800%	261,941	0	584,929	322,563	261,941
5	66	0	0	4.800%	276,166	0	608,326	331,735	276,166
6	67	0	0	4.800%	291,164	0	632,660	341,071	291,164
7	68	0	0	4.800%	306,976	0	657,966	350,565	306,976
8	69	0	0	4.800%	323,647	0	684,285	360,213	323,647
9	70	0	0	4.800%	341,223	0	711,656	370,008	341,223
10	71	0	0	4.800%	359,754	0	740,122	379,944	359,754

End of Year Projection

Voluntary payments

When homeowners provide voluntary payments, they simultaneously reduce the compounding of debt in the loan balance and build up the line of credit.

Table 6.3: *Converting line of credit at age seventy to tenure payments of $605*

	Loan Balance @ 8 Years	Line of Credit @ 8 Years	Equity @ 8 Years
Make Voluntary Payment 62–70	$212,755	$110,892	$471,104
No Voluntary Payment	$322,647	$0	$360,213

This table displays the loan balance, line of credit, and retained equity side by side in cases where voluntary payments are made and not made. Now, what if the client wished to make payments early in retirement from age sixty-two to seventy and then convert to receiving HECM tenure payments?

This couple continued to reduce the loan balance by making voluntary payments. This meant they could stop at any time. But in this plan, the couple built up their line of credit enough by making payments so that when they stopped working at age seventy and took Social Security, they could convert that line of credit to tenure payments of hundreds of dollars per month. What they wanted above all was cash flow to meet the unexpected as they aged. Luckily, they had a savvy financial planner.

Flexible feature four

This feature involves the option of making a final payment at the end in one balloon payment. The HECM permits one balloon payment with no interim payments required. Technically, the balloon is not due until the last participating homeowner dies, moves, or sells.

CASE STUDY: PARENTS AND HEIRS CAN WORK TOGETHER SO THAT THE PARENTS CAN LIVE COMFORTABLY AND STILL CONSERVE THE HOME EQUITY

The homeowner, Mr. Stokes, was eighty-three years old and wanted to renovate his home. He could not qualify for a mortgage based on his ability to make monthly payments. He took a HECM and borrowed just $100,000 for his home upgrades even though he was eligible to borrow more. His daughter worked with him to set up the reverse mortgage and arranged to make voluntary interest payments on the loan balance. If the grandkids needed braces that month, she skipped the payment with no repercussions. This kept the loan balance at around the original $100,000. When Mr. Stokes died, the improved house went to his daughter with a very manageable loan balance. She took out her own mortgage, satisfied the HECM, and moved in with her family.

Flexible feature five

The final flexible feature allows a portion or all of the house to repay the loan. When the last borrower exits the house, that borrower or the estate will choose whether to sell the house and pay back the mortgage *or* through other means (such as arranging traditional financing) pay off the HECM and retain the home. Should the loan balance be greater than the home value, the home alone will satisfy the debt. If the loan amount is less than what the house brings at sale, the borrower or the estate are entitled to the remaining equity.

Conclusion

As discussed, the HECM's flexible lending terms allow borrowers to literally custom design their own mortgages:

- **Option 1:** Treat it as a classic reverse mortgage to be paid back in one balloon payment

- **Option 2:** Use as an I-O loan but without the threat of a future recast requiring principal reduction

- **Option 3:** Repay all draws and fees, except a $100 minimum balance, in order to keep the balance low but the line of credit growing

- **Option 4:** Start with one option but convert to another as needs change in retirement

Any of the above options are allowed and can be changed immediately without consequences. Truly the HECM provides an uncommon level of versatility.

SEVEN

What Happens At Loan's End?

If the borrower(s) die or permanently move from the house, what most borrowers or heirs want to know is how long they have to arrange new financing or sell the house to satisfy the loan balance. Not surprisingly, some fear they will be pushed into a fire sale situation. Yet the process for satisfying the loan is orderly as long as the borrower or heirs stay in communication with the servicer.

Mrs. Owens was a vivacious and erudite eighty-four-year-old when she called about establishing a reverse mortgage. She wanted to extract money from her house to give her son a down payment for his first house. She was so cute that we filmed her for a commercial long after the closing and in doing so she showed us pictures of her swimming with her grandchildren at her son's new house. She was joyful at having shared her wealth with her family while still alive.

A couple of years later, her son Floyd called us to let us know she had died. Floyd was preparing to put his mom's house on the market, and wanted the specifics on handling the reverse mortgage debt. This is where it gets tricky as debtor's remorse can overshadow the utility the mortgage provided. But in this case, Floyd was so grateful for what the reverse mortgage had enabled for both his family and his mother that he actually thanked us for "giving" them a reverse mortgage. We were able to help him find a good Realtor© to help him sell her house and all went smoothly. He was even a little surprised that there was money left over from the sale of the house. That money came to him.

Snowbirds

Some folks are afraid that they will be tied to their homes and that traveling will trigger a due and payable status. Happily, HECM homeowners are not chained to their mortgaged homes. In fact, they are allowed to leave the home periodically as long as they maintain the HECM property as a principal residence. HECM borrowers are permitted to own multiple homes.

When a borrower enters a nursing home

Some are concerned about what happens if one of the borrowers moves to a long-term care facility. As long as one of the eligible borrowers remains in the home, a move to a nursing home by the other is irrelevant. If there is just one homeowner and he or she enters a long-term care facility, the HECM remains in effect for a full year. If that last homeowner does not return to the home within the year, a move is presumed to have taken place, thus triggering a due and payable status.

Death or permanent departure

Upon death or permanent departure of the last remaining participant, the process is as follows:

If the heirs want to keep the house in the family

In this case, the family pays off the HECM mortgage. Just like any other mortgage, the heirs can pay off the reverse mortgage either with cash or by acquiring their own financing. With the HECM, however, they will pay either the current loan balance or 95% of the appraised value, whichever is less.

If the borrower/heirs do not want the house and it is not underwater

The borrower/heirs can sell the property and have up to a year to do so. This interval includes time extensions based on the assumption that the owner/estate is actively working to sell the property or satisfy the debt. They must keep the loan servicer informed and prove the property is listed. Any property sales proceeds in excess of the loan balance belong to the owner/estate. The lender is not entitled to an equity share beyond the ending loan balance. It is in the owner/estate's best interest, however, to complete arrangements quickly, because interest on the loan, as well as MIP charges, continue to accrue.

The reverse mortgage servicer provides a written payoff statement, and at closing, the loan balance is paid off, just as would be the case with any other mortgage. Again, after the loan is paid off, any and all remaining equity goes to the seller, which typically is the borrower's heirs or estate.

If the heirs want the house and it is underwater

In this case, a short sale is arranged. Negotiating is not permitted. The heirs may retire the loan by paying either the current loan balance or 95% of the appraised value, whichever is less.

If the heirs do not want the house and it is underwater

To avoid foreclosure, the estate can execute a deed-in-lieu of foreclosure, which is a voluntary action to deed the collateral property to the servicer in exchange for a release from all obligations under the mortgage. HECM loans are non-recourse; the borrower and the estate *cannot* be held responsible for any shortfall. The house repays what it can, and any shortfall is covered by the FHA insurance fund.

Foreclosure

If the estate does not actively try to sell the property, execute a short sale, or volunteer for a DIL, then there is no choice but to recoup the investment through foreclosure proceedings. Foreclosure must be approved by HUD. The estate is entitled to the copies of the loan history, the name of the current investor, a copy of the loan documents including the mortgage note, deed of trust, and mortgage assignment, which demonstrate the right to foreclose on their loan if no other actions are taken. After a loan is due and payable, the estate benefits by communicating with the servicer to discuss and understand options to avoid foreclosure.

Eligible non-borrowing spouse deferral period

In 2014, FHA gave new status to spouses who are under sixty-two. In the past, a spouse younger than sixty-two could not participate in the loan. When the loan became due, usually at the death of the older spouse, the remaining spouse would either have to move out or attempt to refinance the HECM with his or her own HECM. A refinance was not possible in many cases, especially when a full-draw lump sum had been advanced and/or property values had dropped. Worse, some unscrupulous lenders encouraged couples to drop the younger borrower so they could use the age of the older borrower to create a higher loan balance. (Remember, the older the borrower, the more initial credit is available; if a younger borrower is on the title, the younger birthday is used to determine loan proceeds.)

Younger spouses were forced out of their homes at the death of the older one. Greater consumer safeguards were needed to protect the younger spouse from displacement. In response to this problem, HUD/FHA created the non-borrowing spouse status, which is defined as "...the spouse, as determined by the law of the state in which the spouse and mortgagor (borrower) reside or the state of celebration, of the HECM mortgagor at the time of closing and who also is not a mortgagor."[1]

This new category allows for a deferral period of the due and payable status during which the remaining spouse may continue to occupy the house. Caution: At time of this writing, the deferral period is available only on the death of the mortgagor (borrower) and does not apply if the mortgagor exits the home for another reason.

To achieve NBS status, the spouse must:

* Have been the spouse of a HECM borrower at the time of loan closing and have remained the spouse of the HECM lender for the duration of the HECM borrower's lifetime

* Have been properly disclosed to the lender at origination and specifically named as non-borrowing spouse in the HECM documents

* Have occupied, and continue to occupy, the property securing the HECM as the principal residence of the non-borrowing spouse

* Be able to establish a legal right to remain in the house

HUD/FHA accompanied this change with an expanded table of credit availability (Principal Limit) factors. As always, the factor used is based on the youngest participant. These new factors allow for credit determinants as young as eighteen years old. The initial available cash, of course, is reduced accordingly due to a longer expected lifespan.

In a January 2015 Mortgagee Letter (ML 2015-02), the FHA further defined the eligible non-borrowing spouse as one who can establish a legal right to remain in the home after the death of the principal borrower. This status is different from that of an ineligible non-borrowing spouse. Those ineligible for the deferral period are deemed so because they:

- are not legally married to the borrower

- do not reside in the subject property

- or do not plan to reside in the subject property

When an ineligible NBS is identified, the Principal Limit will be based on the age of the younger HECM borrower or eligible NBS living in the property.

A non-borrowing spouse whose spouse died is subject to strict timelines to establish the right to remain in the home. It is critical that the NBS be in touch with the servicer immediately to be guided through the process. Today an NBS is allowed to "go on title" once the reverse mortgage is in effect. All NBSs are advised to take precautionary steps at the outset of the loan to reduce time in probate in order to meet HUD servicing timelines. Legal advice is strongly recommended.

It is important to note that the NBS will not be entitled to further draws from the reverse mortgage. The couple must plan carefully as the tax, insurance, and maintenance obligations will still need to be met once the borrower dies, but without the assistance of reverse mortgage draws of any kind, including any set-asides that may have been established for that purpose.

In June of 2015, HUD responded to lawsuits regarding former non-borrowing spouses by allowing greater latitude for lenders to assign these loans to HUD.[2] Interpretations of new regulations by lenders often result in more clarification from FHA/HUD. Readers should refer to the most recent mortgagee letters regarding eligible/ineligible NBS status.

If a borrower wants to pay off the HECM but continue living in the house

A borrower who wants to continue living in the house cannot take advantage of an underwater situation by paying off the mortgage using the 95% rule. In choosing to live in the house, the borrower who volunteers to extinguish the HECM would be charged the current loan balance regardless of home value. However, the borrower would not be subject to a prepayment penalty. Once a borrower leaves, he or she maintains the right to present the lender with a deed-in-lieu of foreclosure. Again, leaving the house permanently creates no personal liability for repayment.

Conclusion

HUD/FHA places time constraints on the lender as there is no economic benefit to retaining an unoccupied home. The loan is predicated on actuarial tables, so heirs cannot just move into the house and let the balance continue to accrue. A HECM is not assumable. Arrangements for loan disposition must be made in a reasonable time period.

The clock starts ticking the day the last surviving borrower no longer occupies the property as a primary residence. Once the home is unoccupied, the borrower or the estate has six months to pay off the loan. In addition to the initial six months, up to two three-month extensions can be requested (for a total of one year) if more time is needed.

Extensions are not automatic; documentation that the home is listed for sale, a sale is pending, or a family member is applying for financing on the home, is required for an extension to be granted.

The loan servicer should be contacted immediately once the home is vacant. Reverse mortgage servicers deal with these situations every day and will work with borrowers and family members. However, they can't help if they don't hear from anyone. All reverse mortgage servicers send monthly loan statements to borrowers. Those statements contain all loan and contact information necessary to make contact with the lender.[3]

Notes

1   http://portal.hud.gov/hudportal/documents/huddoc?id=14-
    07ml.pdf.

2   http://portal.hud.gov/hudportal/documents/huddoc?id=15-
    15ml.pdf.

3   Laurie MacNaughton and Neil Sweren,
    "How the Back-End of a Reverse Mortgage Works,"
    Middleburg Reverse Lady blog (October 14, 2014).
    By permission of Laurie MacNaughten.

EIGHT

Can You Really Buy A House Using A Reverse Mortgage?

Advisers, Realtors©, builders, and consumers are surprised to learn that a HECM can be used to buy a new residence. For a period of time, Fannie Mae provided a reverse mortgage, the Home Keeper®, that provided financing at the closing table for home purchase. Yet until the Housing and Economic Recovery Act of 2009, the FHA HECM could only be employed by borrowers already residing in their homes. This caused the borrower who wanted to move to a new house and place a reverse mortgage on it to endure two closings. The process required two steps:

1. Take title to the home (purchase transaction)

2. Acquire the reverse mortgage (refinance transaction)

If borrowers did not have the cash to buy the house outright in the first closing, they bore the expense of obtaining and qualifying for a conventional mortgage in order to complete the purchase. At some point, the borrowers would incur a second set of closing costs when they initiated a reverse mortgage to replace the temporary mortgage.

The FHA rectified this inequity by allowing HECM funds to be disbursed at the purchase closing, thus eradicating the need for a second transaction.

Purchasing a new principal residence versus buying a second home

HECM financing is tied to the homeowner's principal residence. Because there are no limitations on how reverse mortgage funds can be used, it always has been permissible to extract money from the permanent residence to buy a second home. This is common in families where the parents want to continue living in their legacy home but the children prefer to retain the vacation home.

Table 8.1: *Buying a second home with HECM*

HECM Placed on Legacy Home	Calculation Based on $600,000 Home Value
Lump Sum Draw from HECM @ Day 366	$280,000
Beach House Cash Purchase	$280,000
Mortgage on Beach House	$0

The parents used $280,000 in cash from their legacy home to purchase the family beach house. No monthly payments are due on the beach house or the legacy home, although interest and MIP will accrue on the HECM loan balance. The heirs will inherit both houses, sell the legacy home, and retain the vacation spot for future generations.

Compare the above scenario to the purchase of a new principal residence using the HECM:

Table 8.2: *Buy a new principal home using a HECM*

Cost of New Home	$400,000
HECM Lump Sum Draw At Loan Origination	$210,000
Required Down Payment	$190,000
Monthly Mortgage Payment	$0

Notice that the homeowner in this example is able to draw the full lump sum at the closing and does not have to wait until Day 366 to access the entire cash benefit. This is because a HECM purchase transaction is deemed a mandatory obligation and no waiting period is necessary to access the full lump sum. The homeowner purchases the new home by providing a portion of the sale price as cash. The amount required is based on age and current interest rates. This cash down payment becomes equity. Generally this cash comes from the sale of the departure home, but other funds may be used. The remaining purchase funds come in the form of a lump sum reverse mortgage. The homeowners may live in the new house free of payment until the last one dies, moves, or sells.

How HECM purchase money is calculated

It is difficult to envision how the HECM purchase transaction unfolds unless you understand that the reverse mortgage financing attaches to the home being purchased, not to the home being left behind.

The departure home is not used to calculate purchase money funds.

LEGACY HOME

HECM Reverse Mortgage is placed on new home.

This house is used to determine HECM purchase funds. The reverse mortgage attaches to the new principal residence.

NEW RETIREMENT HOME

Figure 8.1: Departure house not part of transaction

Table 8.3: *Formula for determining down payment needed to purchase/examples*

Purchase Price	HECM Lump Sum	Down Payment
$300,000	$180,000	$120,000
$1,000,000	$340,000	$660,000
$700,000	$300,000	$400,000

(Purchase price) – (HECM lump sum)* = Down Payment

*The HECM lump sum draw is calculated using the HECM formula taking into account the age of the youngest borrower or eligible non-borrowing spouse, the current expected interest rate, and the FHA-appraised value of the home or $726,525, whichever is less. Some buyers have reported that they used IRA funds to make the initial down payment. They repaid the IRA money within sixty days by selling the former home and avoided a tax bill.

EXAMPLE A: DOUBLE BUYING POWER

In this case, a widow, Mrs. Bridges, needed to move to a home nearer her children several states away. A Realtor© advised her that her current home would net, after expenses, $150,000. She did not want to mortgage her new home, and even if she applied for a traditional mortgage, she likely would not qualify. She had given up trying to move because the houses near her children cost $250,000 to $300,000. Her $150,000 budget would not be enough to purchase any of those houses.

Her son's financial adviser provided the solution. He advised the family to go ahead and search for a comfortable house in a good neighborhood nearby.

They found a suitable home, all on one level, five minutes from the grandchildren. The house cost $300,000. Mrs. Bridges was able to purchase this house because, at her age, she qualified for a lump sum payment, from a reverse mortgage, of $180,000. Her down payment was just $120,000. This allowed her to save the unspent $30,000 from the sale of her departure home. She moved into the new house and never made a payment on interest or principal.

EXAMPLE B: BUY MORE HOUSE

In this case, the Herberts were drawn to a luxury development in Naples, Florida. They had netted $660,000 from the sale of their legacy home in New Jersey. They were comfortable spending this amount but did not want to dip into savings or take on a mortgage. When they met with the builder, however, they quickly learned that luxury options like a pool, a waterfront lot, a chef's kitchen, spa bathrooms, and other upgrades shot the potential price up to $1 million. The builder knew of the HECM purchase program and was able to calculate that they would qualify for a $340,000 lump sum payment. By combining the HECM-purchase lump-sum money with the $660,000 they already had, the Herberts were able to order all the upgrades they desired. And like Mrs. Bridges, the Herberts never made a payment on interest or principal.

EXAMPLE C: CONSERVE NEST EGG

A financial adviser in Sacramento helped Mr. Chen manage a move to San Francisco to be with his family after his wife died. Mr. Chen sold his house in Sacramento and netted $460,000. He was faced with having to spend $700,000 for his new house in the city. Having lived through his wife's protracted illness, he was sensitive to holding onto as much cash as possible. He could manage the $700,000 purchase but would have to divest $240,000 of his brokerage account to make up the difference. And for Mr. Chen, a traditional mortgage was out of the question.

Both he and his adviser were reluctant to take so much cash out of his nest egg. The adviser calculated that a HECM for Purchase lump sum of $300,000 could be used toward the purchase. Mr. Chen's down payment, then, was $400,000 ($700,000 – 300,000). So instead of using all $460,000 of his proceeds, he saved $60,000 plus the $240,000 that he did not withdraw from his savings.

Table 8.4: Purchase without HECM vs. purchase using HECM purchase money

Purchase without HECM	$700,000 Purchase Price
Net Proceeds from Departure House	$460,000
Portfolio Withdrawal	($240,000)
Purchase using HECM Purchase Money	*$700,000 Purchase Price*
Net Proceeds from Departure House	$460,000
HECM Purchase Money Lump Sum	$300,000
Cash Down Payment from Net Sale Proceeds	*$400,000*
Cash Retained	$240,000 + $60,000 = +$300,000

Until Mr. Chen leaves the house permanently, he will not make a payment on either the interest or the principal. The adviser prepared a new financial plan for Mr. Chen taking into account the positive $300,000 swing in his financial profile. He demonstrated with financial software that Mr. Chen's cash flow survival probabilities were improved dramatically. Even though he was buying an expensive house he was able to manage his fixed monthly expenses by using a HECM for Purchase.

Mr. Chen's adviser compared his retirement chances paying for his house in cash versus using a HECM for Purchase to provide the $300,000 portion of the sales price.

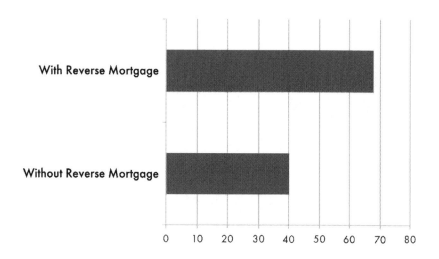

Figure 8.2: *Example of improvement in portfolio success using HECM for Purchase*

Planners can provide graphics comparing one retirement plan versus another. In this case, Mr. Chen's chances of having enough cash flow throughout a long retirement were improved from less than 40% to 68%. (Courtesy of Money Guide Pro.)

EXAMPLE D: BUY A FOURPLEX AND LIVE IN IT FOR RETIREMENT SECURITY

Ted Butler, a reverse mortgage expert in California, contributed this scenario. His client, aged seventy-two, had a home free and clear. He would have been eligible for $1,100 a month on the HECM tenure plan. This was acceptable, but he still worried about his cash flow. Instead, he chose to sell this house and netted $500,000. He reserved $70,000 in savings and used $430,000 as a down payment on a HECM for Purchase transaction on a fourplex. He had no principal or interest obligations. He lived in the deluxe unit and rented out the other three. This netted him $3,000 a month after property management, taxes, and insurance. That $36,000 in income was comforting because the rentals were recession-proof and inflation-proof and were tied to an appreciating asset.

Conclusion

In this chapter we discussed the mechanics of using a reverse mortgage to purchase either a second home or a new principal residence. We touched on a very important consideration: the improvement in cash flow when money is not tied up in either an all-cash purchase or making monthly mortgage payments. In a later chapter we will explore what these options mean in retirement income planning. For now, we have seen that the HECM for Purchase program can benefit the homeowner by:

- Eliminating monthly interest and principal payments, thus improving cash flow

- Doubling the purchasing power for some homes, subject to age and interest rates

- Enabling an upgrade to a more expensive property

- Conserving the nest egg

- Enabling the purchase of a multi-family home to provide personal housing and income

Retirees are strongly drawn to making all-cash purchases because meeting monthly mortgage payments is stressful. But buying a house with all cash can seriously deplete potential savings. A HECM for Purchase contributes to the sense of security so coveted by retirees because it eradicates the monthly mortgage payment and/or a huge cash outlay. A HECM for Purchase provides the look and feel of an all-cash purchase without the pain.

And remember what we learned in Chapter 6. Homeowners can make voluntary payments on the loan balance when convenient in order to keep the loan balance low. This could allow for the house to pay back just what was initially borrowed, while conserving the remaining equity growth.

NINE

Housing Wealth Is Not A Last-Resort Strategy

Now we are going to start looking at numbers. But before going further, let's consider how difficult retirement income planning is. In fact, it is so hard that William F. Sharpe, who won the 1990 Nobel prize in Economics, called retirement-income planning the most complex problem he'd analyzed in his career.[1]

Certainly, this book can do little to help you understand all the factors that can lead to portfolio ruin in retirement. Nevertheless, we can review what the Eggheads, as we affectionately call them, are thinking about the role housing wealth *could* play in retirement.

It all started in 2004 when former physicist turned tax and pension lawyer Barry H. Sacks, from San Francisco, started looking for a way to buffer portfolio volatility in retirement. He was aware of the risks that retirees would face once they moved out of the accumulation phase and started relying on their nest eggs for income. Although we could make an exhaustive list of risks that can affect a retirement, there are core inexorable economic realities that could jeopardize retirement for Baby Boomers: longevity risk, funding risk, sequence of returns risk, and consumption risk.

1. Longevity risk

Documentation abounds for how long the Boomer generation can expect to live. Vanguard cites the Society of Actuaries, which found that if a man and woman are married, the chance that at least one of them will live to any given age is increased. There's a 72% chance that one of them will live to age eighty-five and a 45% chance that one will live to age ninety. There's even an 18% chance that one of them will live to age ninety-five, as shown below.

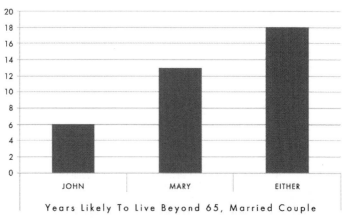

Figure 9.1: *Probability of living a selected number of years*

We just do not know how long our savings must stretch since we do not know how long we will live.

2. 401(k): Risk for funding retirement has shifted to the individual

Traditional pensions are disappearing as a vehicle to fund retirement in America. Beginning with a change to the IRS Code in 1978, the adoption of qualified plans such as the 401(k) have shifted the responsibility of funding retirement away from the employer and onto the shoulders of the individual.

With defined benefit plans (pensions), the employer provides a fixed and guaranteed payment to the retired employees. Yet the *cost* of funding these guarantees is variable and depends on how the pension fund has invested the money needed to make those future payments. So in a traditional pension plan the employer bears the risk of investments for funding the pension plan, trying to keep up with the obligation to make payments to the retired employees. A defined contribution plan, in contrast, specifies the amount the employer will contribute to a retirement account at the employee's direction, and how much an employee receives in retirement will depend on what his or her personal account ultimately is able to provide. The cost for the employer is now fixed, but the benefit to the employee is variable and subject to market returns. No wonder employers wholeheartedly embraced the 401(k) retirement program and replaced their pension arrangements with it. What this means is that the individual retiree, not the employer, has to figure how to make the nest egg last.

Sadly, underfunded pension plans themselves are posing a risk to those who retired expecting a stable pension payment. Moody's Investors Service estimates state and local pensions have unfunded liabilities of about $4 trillion, roughly equal to the economy of Germany, the world's fourth-largest economy. Arun Muralidhar, PhD, describes the weakening guarantees to workers in his book *Fifty States of Gray*. Dr. Muralidhar stipulates that the transfer from defined benefit (pension) plans to defined contribution plans resulted in coverage gaps because many employees just do not participate in the savings opportunity. And the effects of the tech bubble (2000–2002), lower long-term interest rates, and the Great Recession of 2008 reduced the wealth of pension funds, in some cases causing states to reduce benefits to shore up state finances, which threatened retirement security.

Not many Americans can count on a fixed-formula pension arrangement (defined benefit plan) from their employers. Instead, average Americans supposedly have provided for their own retirements by saving earnings over the years in defined contribution plans and then can be expected to invest and spend the funds appropriately.

Not surprisingly, Americans are nervous about whether or not they have saved enough to last throughout a long retirement. AARP reported in 2010 that the fear of running out of money exceeds the fear of death. In fact, when the choice is death or financial ruin, 63% fear money woes more than death.[2] If you are like me, your biggest fear is being a burden on your children. I expect to die but I really hope that I can take care of myself in retirement.

3. Market volatility: Sequence of returns risk and reverse dollar-cost averaging

Bengen Rule: Spend less than the average rate of return

Although planners disagree on the exact level of probability, there is a general acceptance that there is a high probability that an investment portfolio will provide cash payments throughout a thirty-year retirement if the retiree draws from that portfolio an amount that conforms to the "Bengen Rule." The Bengen Rule states that a retiree, in the first year of retirement, may draw about 4% of the portfolio's value at the beginning of retirement and, each year thereafter, draw the same dollar amount, adjusted only for inflation (irrespective of the portfolio's investment performance).

William Bengen demonstrated this rule in a *Journal of Financial Planning* article in 1994, using historical investment performance data. More recently, Monte Carlo testing[3] has shown that a retiree's chances of avoiding portfolio ruin could be 90% if the retiree follows the Bengen Rule, sometimes called the SafeMax. This approach provides for constant purchasing power across the retirement years and thus takes into account the assumption that inflation will impact spending needs. In other words, every year inflation will erode your purchasing power. You just do not know what your profits will be on your savings, so you must be careful to spend less than the average rate of return.

Financial experts have been ratcheting down the 4% figure to somewhere closer to 3.2% which makes it even more difficult to budget in retirement.

But let's take a look at what 4% looks like. If you have a $1 million retirement account at retirement, your withdrawal would be $40,000. Every year after that, under the Bengen Rule, you would take an increase equal to inflation on the original $40,000.

But what if there is a Black Swan event like the Great Recession of 2008 that reduced retirement accounts by 30% or 40%? Do you still want to take your withdrawal from your account and lock in your losses? What if the Black Swan happens early in retirement when you are still trying to plan on having enough money for twenty or thirty more years?

Sequence of returns risk

The order of good to bad returns (profits) on the retirement accounts matters. You just cannot assume that spending below your average rate of return will be safe. So if you are earning an average of 6.8% profit, advisers warn you not to spend the 6.8%. Why? Because if you live long enough, bad days are coming and you must account for that by underspending.

Monte Carlo testing of retirement scenarios

There are thousands of possible lifetime outcomes for any individual retirement plan. These outcomes are dependent on variables such as inflation, asset allocation, consumption needs, and market volatility. Your financial adviser will test the plan by simulating potential changes in the variables. They do this with a Monte Carlo simulation. The computer program tests a myriad of possible future ups and downs in the factors that affect your savings. From calculating all the possible outcomes, some results will fail to provide income for a thirty-year retirement but others will do so handsomely. So, for any one plan the Monte Carlo analysis calculates a probability of success. If 90% of the possible outcomes resulted in a positive retirement account at thirty years, then the probability of success is 90%. Because we cannot know the future, we can only state what percentage of possible outcomes survived for the entire retirement.

In this testing, the retiree's retirement plan portfolio will be subjected to especially bad sequences of investment returns. These could happen early in retirement or the negative profits could persist for a long time. Generally, this phenomenon is particularly dangerous if the bad returns occur in the early years of retirement.

If the early portfolio returns are low or negative, there is long-term impact on the portfolio size. Think about it. If you aim to take out just 4% on your $1 million investment the first year of retirement in order to account for unknown future volatility, you will draw $40,000. But imagine that just before your first-year withdrawal, your portfolio drops from $1 million to $700,000. Your $40,000 draw would represent not the relatively safe 4%, but rather 5.71%. If returns are bad again the next year, you would be compounding the problem. You will take a large chunk out of an already reduced portfolio. Once shares are sold, they are gone forever and cannot participate in an eventual market recovery.

To illustrate how dangerous it is to spend from your savings in a bear market, Thornburg Investment Management prepared a paper describing how the order of portfolio returns on investment can affect portfolio survival:

> Sequence of returns is simply the order in
> which returns are realized by a retiree.
> The consequences of a bad sequence of returns,
> especially early in retirement, can mean
> premature depletion of the portfolio. Retirees
> need to avoid being in the position of having to
> sell during inopportune market environments.

The "average return for this twenty-year period was 8.43%. Reverse the sequence, 2008–1989, and once again, the average annual return is 8.43%!" In fact, if the portfolio is neither added to nor drawn from during the time period under examination, the order of the returns does not affect the average annual return or the amount in the portfolio at the end of the time period. However, "for retirees taking systematic withdrawals, the order in which they realize their returns is crucial to the long-term sustainability of the retirement portfolio."

Table 9.1: S&P 500 Index with inverted sequence of returns

Year	S & P 500 1989–2008 Sequence	S & P 500 2008–1989 Sequence
1	31.69	-37.00
2	-3.11	5.49
3	30.47	15.84
4	7.62	4.91
5	10.08	10.88
6	1.32	28.68
7	37.58	-22.10
8	22.96	-11.88
9	33.36	-9.11
10	28.58	21.04
11	21.04	28.58
12	-9.11	33.36
13	-11.88	22.96
14	-22.10	37.58
15	28.68	1.32
16	10.88	10.08
17	4.91	7.62
18	15.84	30.47
19	5.49	-3.11
20	-37.00	31.69
Average rate of return	8.43%	8.43%

Source: S&P 500

To demonstrate that phenomenon, Thornburg then applied the two different sets of returns, with identical average rates of returns, to a hypothetical portfolio from which the retiree is taking withdrawals. The difference in portfolio values at the end of twenty years is almost $3 million.

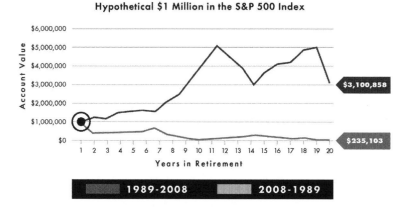

Figure 9.2: *Sequence of returns impact on a hypothetical $1 million investment with retiree taking withdrawals (5% initial rate, 3% inflation), $50,000 first year*

Source: Standard and Poor's and Bureau of Labor Statistics, calculated by Thornburg Investment Management. $50,000 was withdrawn in year one; withdrawal amount was increased by the change in the Consumer Price Index (CPI-U) each year (3.05% average for the period).

The portfolio is invested 100% in equities represented by the S&P 500 Index. As you can see from the chart, after twenty years in retirement, the 1989–2008 sequence has supported the retirement spending and allowed the account value to grow to over $3.1 million. However, the results for the 2008–1989 sequence are quite different. The negative 37% performance in year one followed by significant negative returns in years seven, eight, and nine dramatically deteriorated the account value to approximately $235,000 at the end of the twenty-year period.

Reverse dollar-cost averaging

In the accumulation phase while saving for retirement, most of us take advantage of dollar-cost averaging by making systematic buys. This is what we do as 401(k) participants when we devote a set portion of our paycheck to a contribution. No matter what the market is doing, we continue to buy without regard to market values. We are not trying to time the market but are adhering to a "buy and hold" strategy. Over the course of our earning years, we will have paid top dollar for some of our assets when the market was hot. Conversely, we would have bought some of them greatly discounted when the market was in the bear portion of its volatility cycle. Say you are contributing $100 per paycheck. Sometimes that $100 will not buy you much, but when the market declines your $100 will buy you more units *per dollar invested*. At the end of forty years, your numerous discounted assets are likely to have risen to normal values and thus will contribute significantly to your savings portfolio value over time.

When we retire, we leave the accumulation phase and enter the distribution phase, and the opposite happens. Now we are selling our assets on a regular schedule to meet our spending goals. When the market is hot we sell fewer units to raise the money we need, but in a bear market we must divest more units to raise the cash we need. This outcome violates a universal rule of investing: buy low and sell high.

CASE STUDY

A simplified hypothetical example illustrates reverse dollar-cost averaging. Mr. and Mrs. Hail were using Uber shares to provide monthly income beyond what their Social Security benefits and small pension contributed. At the beginning of their retirement, their Uber stock was selling for $1,000 per share. They needed about $1,000 a month. So they sold one share per month. Then the market tanked, and on top of it Uber ran into regulatory issues. The share price declined to $250. Now Mr. and Mrs. Hail had to sell *four* shares per month, and once those shares were sold, they were gone for good. They locked in their losses by having no choice but to sell in a bear market.

Over a thirty-year retirement, reverse dollar-cost averaging can put a nest egg in jeopardy. Thornburg demonstrates this effect on a hypothetical portfolio over five years. When share prices drop for the Not Optimal portfolio (see Tables 9.2 and 9.3 opposite), many more shares have to be sold to raise the $50,000 the retiree needs. Over this period, 31,032 shares were sold due to bear market conditions versus only 23,569 shares sold in the Optimal order of returns.

Table 9.2: *Optimal reverse dollar-cost averaging*

Year	Share Price	Withdrawal Amount	Shares Sold
Beginning	$10		
1	$10	-$50,000	-$5,000
2	$12	-$50,000	-$4,167
3	$13	-$50,000	-$3,846
4	$9	-$50,000	-$5,556
5	$10	-$50,000	-$5,000

Initial Share Value	$10.00	
Average Share Price	$10.80	
Total Shares Sold		-$23,569

Table 9.3: *Not Optimal reverse dollar-cost averaging*

Year	Share Price	Withdrawal Amount	Shares Sold
Beginning	$10		
1	$10	-$50,000	-$5,000
2	$6	-$50,000	-$8,333
3	$7	-$50,000	-$7,143
4	$9	-$50,000	-$5,556
5	$10	-$50,000	-$5,000

Initial Share Value	$10.00	
Average Share Price	$8.40	
Total Shares Sold		-$31,032

The above tables are designed to demonstrate the mathematical principle behind reverse dollar-cost averaging. The illustrations are hypothetical and are not intended to serve as a projection of the investment results of any particular investment.

4. Consumption and the risk of declining purchasing power

Whether or not we adhere to a budget is sometimes voluntary and sometimes not. There are so many potential expenses in retirement that can derail even the most parsimonious spender. Dental expenses, hearing aids, uninsured medical expenses, car repairs, home repairs, and long-term care convalescence are just a few risks to consumption that are extremely hard to anticipate. The most unforgiving of all is severe inflation.

Model of inflation shortfall assuming fixed income of $1,341 per month* and expenses beginning at $1,341 then rising with stated inflation rate over a 20-year retirement period

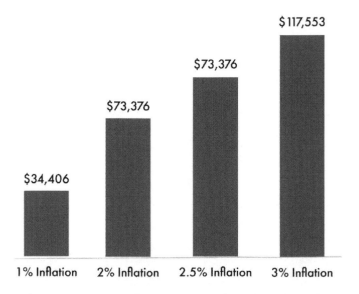

			$117,553
		$73,376	
	$73,376		
$34,406			
1% Inflation	2% Inflation	2.5% Inflation	3% Inflation

*-$1,341 is average monthly Social Security benefit, as of Jan. 2016

Figure 9.3: *Impact of inflation on purchasing power*
Source: LIMRA Secure Retirement Institute

Even a low rate of inflation can significantly erode purchasing power in the long run. LIMRA Secure Retirement Institute modeled the effect that 2% annual inflation could have on a twenty-year retirement. Using a fixed monthly income of $1,341 (the average monthly benefit paid by Social Security) and assuming that monthly expenses increase from $1,341 to $1,993 at the end of the twenty-year period, the inflationary impact results in a shortfall of $73,376. When the calculation is run at 3% inflation, the shortfall jumps to more than $117,000.[4]

Given the headwinds a long retirement will encounter:

- Will retirees be willing or even able to live comfortably on a budget that limits their spending to a withdrawal rate that is sustainable for thirty to forty years—i.e., 4% or less, especially with high inflation?

- Will retirees adjust to market volatility and scale back consumption when market returns are weak or negative?

So there we have it: finite resources, unknown longevity, volatile economic conditions. Something had to give! Barry Sacks, an MIT physicist and Harvard-trained tax and pension lawyer, was thinking about how difficult it would be to maintain cash flow over a long retirement. What could be done to protect the nest egg?

Barry Sacks: How a reverse mortgage protects cash flow

In 2004, Dr. Sacks introduced a new concept in reverse mortgage lending. In doing so he revamped the way a reverse mortgage could be used. Traditionally, reverse mortgages were left as a last resort, to be considered only if and when retirees had exhausted their other assets. Dr. Sacks turned this concept on its head. He studied using the reverse mortgage, selectively, during the entire course of retirement. He wanted to avoid unfavorable results from a bad sequence of portfolio returns, and the impact of reverse dollar-cost averaging. As we have seen, these phenomena are dangerous to Boomers managing their own retirement incomes because periods of market volatility are certain to happen during a longer retirement.

Dr. Sacks perceived that the house is another asset that could provide cash flow in retirement. Could this asset be a resource that could substitute temporarily for portfolio draws? Could a reverse mortgage be used in coordination with portfolio withdrawals throughout retirement? In other words, would the reverse mortgage help protect the client's portfolio in bear markets? (And, Dr. Sacks noted, unlike securities, which generally need to be sold in order to provide income, and hence are gone once they are sold, a reverse mortgage does not diminish the continuing shelter and enjoyment of the home. You may be consuming some of your house value with a reverse mortgage, but you still get to live in the whole house.)

To test his theory, Dr. Sacks compared 5,000 possible outcomes with two identical simulated portfolios, based on historical rates of return. The first portfolio was drawn upon until exhausted. The second portfolio used reverse mortgage line of credit draws instead of portfolio draws following bear markets. These reverse mortgage draws enabled the homeowner to avoid having to sell securities when they were undervalued. An example illustrating the results of this kind of test is shown in the table below. (Note that the 6.5% initial rate is dramatically higher than the typical 4% rate that most planners budget.)

Table 9.4: Integrating reverse mortgage in retirement distribution over 30 years

Draw Source	Remaining Portfolio	Remaining Net Worth Including Housing Wealth
Portfolio until exhausted, then reverse mortgage when and if portfolio is exhausted	Zero balance remains in 35% of trials	Range depending on thousand of hypothetical investment returns: $600,000–$12 million
Portfolio except substitute using draws from reverse mortgage allowing portfolio to recover in years following bear markets	Zero balance remains in 14% of trials	Range: $1.1 to 13.9 million

$1 million (60% stock and 40% fixed income) portfolio drawn at 6.5% initial rate draw adjusted yearly for inflation, initial home value $1 million appreciating at 4% historical market data, 5,000 trials.

These results suggested that even with a high 6.5% withdrawal rate, there was less probability that the portfolio would be exhausted (35% failure versus 14% failure) if reverse mortgage draws replaced portfolio spending in years following a bear market. Dr. Sacks concluded his first study with the observation that the use of the Coordinated Strategy generally increases the mean value of the retiree's overall net worth at later times, even though the home equity may be lower than it might be if the Coordinated Strategy is not used.

Results from his initial investigation encouraged Dr. Sacks to pursue the idea of coordinating the housing asset with the portfolio. Rather than rely on establishing a reverse mortgage after the portfolio is exhausted, it appeared that a better use would be to set up a reverse mortgage *early* in retirement and then draw from it strategically when portfolio returns did not provide the needed payout.

CASE STUDY: THE TALE OF TWO HECMS

This case study described by Barry Sacks, PhD, JD and Mary Jo Lafaye compares the fortunes of two retirees who start retirement with identical securities portfolios, receive identical amounts of retirement income throughout a thirty-year retirement, and live in identical homes. The study illustrates how a securities portfolio—such as a 401(k) account or a rollover IRA—that provides retirement income can be substantially helped by a reverse mortgage credit line. More specifically, when the credit line is used in coordination with the portfolio, instead of as a last resort, it prolongs the life of the portfolio and greatly increases the net worth (and the legacy) of the retiree. In this case study, the homeowner on the left in the figure below has used the "last resort" strategy; he has exhausted his portfolio in his 24th year of a thirty-year retirement and has built up a debt of nearly $539,000 against his home by the end of that thirty-year retirement.

By contrast, the borrower on the right has used the Coordinated Strategy; he has a portfolio with more than $1 million at the end of a thirty-year retirement and a debt of about $692,000 against his home. Thus, at the end of the thirty-year retirement, he has a net worth that is more than $900,000 greater than if he had used the uncoordinated strategy, even though both retirees started in identical financial situations and received identical amounts of retirement income.

The Coordinated Strategy is very simple: in each year directly following a year of negative investment returns in the portfolio, the portfolio is not drawn upon. Instead, the reverse mortgage credit line is drawn upon for the retiree's income. In this strategy, the reverse mortgage credit line is used to offset the "adverse sequence of returns."

Table 9.5: Conventional, "Last Resort" Method (draw from reverse mortgage LOC after portfolio is drained) vs. "New Wisdom" method (draw from reverse mortgage LOC following down market)

Year	Conventional Thinking: Last Resort Draw from Portfolio until Depleted					New Wisdom: Coordinate with Investments Draw from LOC Following Down Market				
	Portfolio at Start of Year	Investment Performance	Draw from Portfolio	Draw from RM LOC	Portfolio at End of Year	Portfolio at Start of Year	Investment Performance	Draw from Portfolio	Draw from RM LOC	Portfolio at End of Year
1973	500,000	-9.3%	27,500		428,652	500,000	-9.3%	27,500		428,652
1974	428,652	-15.5%	28,463		338,120	428,652	-15.5%		28,463	362,166
1975	338,120	22.3%	29,459		377,493	362,166	22.3%		29,459	442,932
1976	377,493	17.9%	30,490		409,013	442,932	17.9%	30,490		486,145
1977	409,013	-4.1%	31,557		361,905	486,145	-4.1%	31,557		435,859
1978	361,905	2.2%	32,661		338,552	435,859	2.2%		32,661	445,515
1979	336,552	8.0%	33,805		326,998	445,535	8.0%	33,805		444,710
1980	326,998	15.4%	34,988		337,009	444,710	15.4%	34,988		472,861
1981	337,009	-1.4%	36,212		296,706	472,861	-1.4%	36,212		430,710
1982	296,706	25.2%	37,480		324,655	430,710	25.2%		37,480	539,422
1983	324,655	13.3%	38,791		323,941	539,422	13.3%	38,791		567,314
1984	323,941	8.9%	40,149		308,935	567,314	8.9%	40,149		573,872
1985	308,935	25.2%	41,554		334,734	573,872	25.2%	41,554		666,408
1986	334,734	15.2%	43,009		336,068	666,408	15.2%	43,009		718,156
1987	336,068	3.4%	44,514		301,496	718,156	3.4%	44,514		696,613
1988	301,496	10.3%	46,072		281,809	696,613	10.3%	46,072		717,742
1989	281,809	20.9%	47,685		283,150	717,742	20.9%	47,685		810,367
1990	283,150	1.0%	49,354		236,087	810,367	1.0%	49,354		768,472
1991	236,087	21.4%	51,081		224,524	768,472	21.4%	51,081		870,625
1992	224,524	5.6%	52,869		181,268	870,625	5.6%	52,869		863,551
1993	181,268	7.9%	54,719		136,559	863,551	7.9%	54,719		872,810
1994	136,559	-2.8%	56,634		77,718	872,810	-2.8%	56,634		793,650
1995	77,718	25.7%	58,617		24,007	793,650	25.7%		58,617	997,459
1996	24,007	11.1%	24,007	36,661	0	997,459	11.1%	60,668		1,040,493
1997	0	19.3%	0	62,791	0	1,040,493	19.3%	62,792		1,165,909
1998	0	17.0%	0	64,989	0	1,165,909	17.0%	64,989		1,287,967
1999	0	7.8%	0	67,264	0	1,287,967	7.8%	67,264		1,315,795
2000	0	-0.9%	0	69,618	0	1,315,795	-0.9%	69,618		1,234,712
2001	0	-3.7%	0	72,005	0	1,234,712	-3.7%		72,055	1,189,275
2002	0	-8.6%	0	74,576	0	1,189,275	-8.6%		74,577	1,086,997
	End Balances:		$538,773	$0			End Balances:		$692,007	$1,086,997

-$538,773 Net

+$394,991 Net

+$933,764 Differential to Estate

The investment returns used in the study are those of a real balanced portfolio, specified in widely distributed publicity materials by a nationally known investment management and financial planning firm. The constant purchasing power draw rate is, at the outset, 5.5% of the initial portfolio value. (The assumed inflation rate is a constant 3.5%.) The 5.5% draw rate is well above the so called "4% rule;" therefore, without the reverse mortgage credit line, there was a greater than 40% likelihood that the portfolio would be exhausted in thirty years, and a likelihood of approximately 30% that the portfolio would be exhausted in twenty-five years.

Although this case study is only one example, we can produce (and have produced) thousands of other examples using Monte Carlo simulation. In the overwhelming majority of the examples produced by the simulation, the results are similar to those of this case study. That is, the Coordinated Strategy results in a far greater probability of cash flow survival throughout a thirty-year retirement, and a high probability of a far greater net worth (or legacy) at the end of that retirement, than does the "last resort" strategy.

Notice that four of the first nine years of retirement are in bear territory. This illustration exhibits the danger of encountering adverse returns early in retirement and how substituting draws from the HECM allows the portfolio to participate in the market recovery.

Conclusion

Once a stock is sold, it is gone forever and will not be there to help fund retirement. Spending from the portfolio is especially dangerous in the early years of retirement when care must be taken to draw down a safe percentage. Taking too much will not allow the portfolio to recover and then participate in the compounding growth that will be needed in later years. The essence of the Coordinated Strategy? Don't feed the bear!

Notes

1 www.advisorperspectives.com/newsletters14/Bill_Sharpe_on_
Retirement_Planning.php.

2 "Between the adoption of individual retirement accounts in 1974 and the 401(k) in 1981, the way people planned and invested for retirement began to change. Faced with selecting investments for retirement accounts, the changes caused by the Tax Reform Act in 1986, and a stock market that began to take off in 1982, more people realized they needed help with their financial lives." http://money.com/money/3581647/retirement-savings-outlive-death-worse.

3 A Monte Carlo simulation is a mathematical tool that offers a way to evaluate a particular retirement portfolio. With the help of computer software, a planner can simulate hundreds or thousands of market-condition scenarios and learn the probability that your portfolio would last your expected lifetime.

4 Data from LIMRA.

TEN

When To Draw Strategically From A Reverse Mortgage

In 2012, Dr. Sacks and his brother Stephen R. Sacks, PhD (a retired professor of Economics) published an article in the *Journal of Financial Planning* expanding the original reverse mortgage theory and demonstrating that coordinating housing wealth via a reverse mortgage significantly increases cash flow survival probability throughout retirement. A few months later, John Salter, PhD, CFP®, AIFA®; Shaun Pfeiffer; and Harold Evensky, CFP®, AIF® of Texas Tech University published an article in the same journal. Although they took a slightly different approach, their conclusions validated the Sacks' results: Using a reverse mortgage as a standby line of credit (accessing it to substitute for portfolio draws when the market is down) is a powerful cash flow survival tool. Since 2012 other investigators have published case studies demonstrating that a reverse mortgage, distributed in various methods, can play a key role in retirement planning. To understand various uses, it is important to know how HECM draws can be structured:

- A lump sum

- A term payment

- A tenure payment

- A line of credit

- A combination

Lump sum and mandatory obligations

The homeowner may choose to take an initial lump sum if he or she meets certain requirements known as mandatory obligations. As a result of changes on October 2, 2017, the upfront fee on taking a full draw at closing is reduced from 2.5% of the home value to 2.0%. We have seen that the lump sum can be used in this fashion to purchase a new principal residence (HECM for Purchase).

Pay off traditional mortgage

The most common lump sum disbursal involves replacing a current mortgage with a HECM. With a HECM replacement, monthly household debt payment is reduced. Analysts are interested in how replacing debt with a HECM can affect a retiree's securities portfolio in retirement.

For example, at age sixty-six, when Mrs. Connelly's husband died, she was saddled with a mortgage she could not afford. Her home was a mecca for family gatherings, so she did not want to move out of her neighborhood, far away from her grandchildren. She did have a $750,000 nest egg but her current expenses were $6,000 a month, including $1,200 in principal and interest payments on her mortgage. Her planner understood her predicament and suggested that she replace her mortgage with a HECM.

The adviser demonstrated that, if her portfolio returned 6% yearly for the remainder of her life, her spending (including her mortgage payments and with her other expenses adjusted for inflation at 3% yearly) would exhaust the portfolio by the time she reached age eighty-nine. If, however, she replaced the mortgage with a reverse mortgage, thus reducing her initial spending needs to $4,800 a month, her portfolio, under the same assumptions, survives. And it would still be worth $115,873 when she reached age 100. (This projection does not account for market volatility. In reality, no diversified securities portfolio yields a steady rate of return year after year. Nonetheless, it provides a useful illustration.)

There is a useful calculator illustrating how a retirement scenario is improved by exchanging a mortgage for a HECM at http://rfslends.com/portfolio-without-mortgage-payment.

Of course, the foregoing comparisons favor the outcome using the reverse mortgage because an otherwise unused asset has been put to work to reduce monthly expenses. So in a sense, they are apples-to-oranges comparisons.

A more helpful comparison, more directly apples to apples, is the comparison between the cash flow survival probability when the reverse mortgage is used in a coordinated manner (as described by either the Sackses or by Prof. Salter et al.) versus the cash flow survival probability when the reverse mortgage is used only as a last resort.

Encore career

Others have found that they could start a second (encore) career or business by funding their capital needs with a HECM. The fact that they are not making payments can translate into a competitive advantage as they build the business. Once they have established cash flow, they can pay down/off the HECM without penalty.

Term payment

Sometimes a family may need to extract as much money per month from their HECM as they can in order to pay for in-home health care. The HECM allows for a term payment. Once the term is up there are no more draws allowed, but the loan stays in place until the last participating borrower dies, moves, or sells.

In 2002, Mr. and Mrs. Williams lived in an expensive Bethesda, MD home. They faced significant bills when they chose to keep Mr. Williams at home as he struggled with a life-ending illness. They needed as much money per month as they could access to fund his care. Mrs. Williams was quite a bit younger than her husband, so she elected to go off title to allow them to use his birthdate to calculate the available funds. The HECM term plan easily met this $8,000-a-month cost and, in this case, the term did last until Mr. Williams died.

This was an interesting case because Mrs. Williams had gone off title. (Today's HUD rules will not allow a scenario like this.) After Mr. Williams died, she would have had to move or arrange her own financing to settle the HECM debt. Luckily, this couple had an adept financial planner. A life insurance policy was in place to protect Mrs. Williams. She elected to sell the Bethesda house and retain the remaining equity. She moved to their vacation home in Boca Raton and used the sale proceeds from the Bethesda property and the money from the insurance policy to strengthen her retirement.

Tenure payment: A cash flow floor like an annuity

Sometimes homeowners just want to know that they will receive a dependable stream of mailbox money every month for as long as they live. Tom Hegna is persuasive about the preference people have for guaranteed income, yet most are reluctant to invest in annuities that provide that paycheck every month. In his series, *Don't Worry, Retire Happy* for PBS, he laments that most people are living a "just in case" retirement, saving for a rainy day rather than creating a stream of guaranteed income. The HECM allows for a guaranteed cash flow via the tenure payment. This option allows the borrower to "annuitize" the home equity.

How the HECM Tenure is different than an annuity

Rather than withdrawing cash to purchase an annuity, the HECM borrower uses the housing wealth to accomplish this purpose. By using housing wealth to purchase this tenure annuity, more assets stay invested to continue producing investment returns. This strategy allows more assets to remain in the market, a planning mantra. And of course, while the housing wealth is used to purchase the tenure annuity, the homeowner still retains the full shelter and enjoyment of the house.

An annuity relies on the early deaths of others in the annuitant pool to provide the income promised when an annuity is purchased. These mortality credits are essential but often rub consumers the wrong way. They just don't want to see their investment end up with someone else if they die early. This cannot happen with a HECM. If the borrower sets up a tenure payment and dies early, the remaining equity is still intact and belongs to the heirs. In other words, you cannot lose it if you don't use it!

Caution: A HECM annuity differs from a traditional annuity in another important aspect. The housing annuity (tenure payment) ends when the last borrower leaves the house permanently. A HECM annuity payment is not portable. This is an important feature to consider if a client's other resources are limited. Also of note is that a HECM annuity and other annuities can coexist. Using a traditional annuity does not prevent a homeowner from using a HECM, as well.

Annuities and the HECM can coexist

This statement is worth repeating because there is increasing interest in the idea that retirees would do well to cover their fixed expenses with what Steve Vernon, FSA, in his excellent book *Retirement Game-Changers*, terms "Retirement Paychecks." He suggests creating a "Personal Pension" from both an annuity and a HECM tenure program. The idea is to cover all mandatory monthly expenses with a reliable cash flow stream, and fund discretionary expenses with assets that are invested but are subject to volatile returns.

CASE STUDY: REDUCE PORTFOLIO DRAWS WITH HECM TENURE PAYMENTS

Mr. and Mrs. Grant of Carmel, CA wanted to supplement their retirement income with a monthly guaranteed payment. They were able to create a monthly annuity from their home of $1,715.39 based on an initial credit limit (Principal Limit) of $295,500 on a $500,000 property. In doing so, they were able to leave a $240,000 brokerage account invested. As long as one of them was living in the house as a principal residence, this payment arrived month after month, year after year. They liked the security of knowing that they had baseline income, a floor below which their revenue stream provided by Social Security, and by their house, would not fall. There are numerous calculators online that will illustrate how keeping that $240,000 could provide returns to help finance retirement.

Table 10.1: *How $240,000 will grow to $769,712.56 over 20 years*

Results Summary	
Starting Amount	$240,000
Years	20 years
NO ADDITIONAL CONTRIBUTIONS	$0
Rate of Return	6% compounded annually
Total Interest Earned on Original Investment	$529,712.56
TOTAL SAVED	$769,712.56
Opportunity Cost	$769,712.56

Source: Dinkytown.com

In this hypothetical example, the Grant household was able to stay invested and watch their $240,000 grow to $769,000. Again, this is an apple-to-oranges comparison because the HECM will accrue interest and reduce housing equity. The portfolio grew, but debt on the house grew as well. What is that cost?

"Orderly Draw Down of Home Equity" (Dr. Barbara Stucki)

All HECM lenders can produce an amortization schedule predicting what the cost of the HECM reverse mortgage would be over the same term (Figure 10.2). Whether or not it makes sense to use a HECM to allow a borrower to retain the portfolio longer includes assessing the cost of depleting home equity to do so. For those with a bequest motive, it is important to ask whether or not the heirs would prefer inheriting a house or an investment portfolio. The answer to this may depend on how unified the heirs are on selling the house and dividing those proceeds.

CASE STUDY: THE 6% RULE

Dr. Gerald Wagner, a Harvard PhD and an expert in both reverse mortgages and portfolio theory, published a paper in the *Journal of Financial Planning* in December 2013, investigating how tenure payment supplements can provide greater spending success, particularly in higher tax rate locales. For a sixty-three-year-old borrower living in a $450,000 home and having an $800,000 retirement portfolio, if the first year's withdrawal need is 6.0%, the amount withdrawn is $48,000—i.e., $4,000 a month.

Dr. Wagner explains that:

> [After] paying federal and California taxes, this leaves the homeowner with $2,583 to spend. If the client chooses a HECM tenure payment, there is $1,328 tax-free each month from the HECM. On a tax equivalent basis, that is $2,057, so to meet the desired portfolio withdrawal of $4,000, only $1,943 needs to be withdrawn from the portfolio each month during the first year. Because the HECM tenure advance is fixed, the monthly portfolio withdrawal in the second year will be $2,043. The $100

increase over the first-year accounts for the 2.5% expected annual inflation. Depending on the relative values of the home and portfolio, withdrawal rates of 5.0% to 6.0% can be achieved with over a 90% chance of success over thirty years.

For retirees who are unable to budget at an initial withdrawal rate of 4% (or less), supplementing with a reverse mortgage may provide enough additional income so that their spending needs are met and their portfolio is sufficiently protected to survive for thirty years or more.

Table 10.2: The 6% rule

Scheduled Monthly Draw from HECM	Retirement Horizon	Initial Withdrawal Rate	Probability of Success	Outcome
N/A, Portfolio Draws Only	30 years	4%	90%	Spending Limited
Portfolio Alone	30 years	6%	36%	Not Reliable
Monthly Tenure Supplements from HECM	30 years	6%	90% +	Greater Spending
Portfolio Alone	37 years	3.25%	90%	Spending Limited
Monthly Tenure Supplements from Tenure	37 years	5.5%	90.6%	Longevity Protection

63-year-old client, $800,000 portfolio, minimum 60% equities, $450,000 initial home value, 2014 HECM parameters

Line of credit: The shock absorber

When homeowners establish a HECM as a line of credit, they are gaining access to housing wealth which will be available at any time in the future. This LOC has a truly unusual and remarkable feature: The amount available to be borrowed (to the extent not yet borrowed) grows each month. The rate at which the amount of the LOC not yet borrowed grows is equal to the sum of the monthly interest rate charged on any loan balance outstanding (most servicers require a minimum loan balance of $100) *plus* one-twelfth of the ongoing MIP rate (recently reduced to 0.50% or 0.041 per month). This feature cannot be canceled; it is a contractual obligation made by the lender to the borrower and is insured by the FHA.

As explained by Dr. Wagner in his December 2013 *Journal of Financial Planning* article, "The growing line-of-credit feature maintains the borrowing capacity regardless of when the mortgage is accessed." (This example was calculated before the reduction in ongoing MIP to 0.50% but the concept is the same.)

> For example, with a note rate of 2.50% and an ongoing MIP of 1.25% per annum, a loan's effect rate would be 3.75%. Imagine two borrowers, each with an initial $100,000 line of credit. One draws his entire line of credit at the end of the first year; after one year the capacity would have grown [with monthly compounding] to $103,815. The other borrower lets her line of credit capacity grow untouched for five years. After five years,

the first borrower would owe $120,588. That is $103,815 in principal and $16,773 in accrued interest and MIP. The second borrower could owe nothing and have a line of credit capacity of $120,588. If she then withdrew her whole line of credit, both borrowers would have exactly the same outstanding loan balance.

The growing HECM LOC impressed Dr. John Salter and Harold Evensky, CFP®, of Texas Tech University, for the following reasons:

- The HECM LOC cannot be canceled

- The HECM LOC cannot be frozen

- The HECM LOC cannot be reduced

- The HECM LOC will grow in value even if the housing value drops

Dr. Salter and Harold Evensky, known as the "Dean of Financial Planning," along with Dr. Shaun Pfeiffer, began a series of studies on how the HECM LOC could function as a standby LOC to meet volatility challenges throughout retirement. All lenders are equipped to provide amortization schedules illustrating anticipated LOC growth. These schedules, however, cannot provide a totally accurate prediction of LOC growth because it is not possible to predict what interest rates will be in the future. Because HECMs with the LOC feature use adjustable rates, the loan balance will be charged a varying rate when the underlying index moves up or down. The borrower should take care to negotiate the lowest possible interest rate margin. Interested homeowners may wish to request multiple amortization schedules over a range of potential future interest rates. The borrower can choose either yearly adjusting rates or monthly adjusting rates.

Every lender can provide a schedule displaying the effect of the reverse mortgage on retained equity. Below is an example of an amortization schedule for a borrower who wished to start with a $100,000 line of credit. She was able to establish that LOC and had enough equity left over to take monthly draws for the next twenty years of $659.55. This helped her cash flow, especially to offset her real estate tax obligations. At the end of ten years, her line of credit is projected to have grown to $181,803. Note that in the the last column, her projected remaining home equity is still $604,351. The lower ongoing costs in both lender margins and a reduced MIP contributed to the positive equity. She can either leave the line of credit in place (and growing) or continue to draw on it for cash flow.

Table 10.3: Amortizations schedule showing $100,000 LOC/term draws $659.55 per month, Courtesy of Kerry McKinney

Yr	Age	SVS Fee	Cash Payment	MIP	Rate	Interest	Loan Balance	Line of Credit	Property Value	Equity
1	65	$0	$7,915	$123	4.550%	$1,117	$28,878	$115,512	$520,000	$491,122
2	66	$0	$7,915	$170	4.550%	$1,543	$38,505	$121,483	$540,800	$502,295
3	67	$0	$7,915	$219	4.550%	$1,991	$48,630	$127,762	$562,432	$513,802
4	68	$0	$7,915	$271	4.550%	$2,463	$59,277	$134,365	$584,929	$525,652
5	69	$0	$7,915	$325	4.550%	$2,959	$70,476	$141,310	$608,326	$537,851
6	70	$0	$7,915	$382	4.550%	$3,480	$82,253	$148,613	$632,660	$550,407
7	71	$0	$7,915	$443	4.550%	$4,028	$94,639	$156,295	$657,966	$563,327
8	72	$0	$7,915	$506	4.550%	$4,605	$107,664	$164,373	$684,285	$576,620
9	73	$0	$7,915	$573	4.550%	$5,212	$121,364	$172,868	$711,656	$590,292
10	74	$0	$7,915	$643	4.550%	$5,850	$135,771	$181,803	$740,122	$604,351

Thomas C. B. Davison, PhD, CFP, a Charter Member of the Funding Longevity Task Force, blogs on retirement issues at www.toolsforretirementplanning.com. In the above chart he demonstrates the growth in the HECM LOC at 4% and compares it to the HELOC. The HECM LOC is always growing at the same rate as the loan balance which is the interest rate +0.50% MIP. Note that the higher the rate charged on the HECM loan balance, the faster the HECM LOC will grow.

Both the HELOC and the HECM LOC start with a $200,000 limit. The HECM LOC continues to grow at 4%. The HELOC starts at $200,000 and lasts until the draw period ends at ten years. This example illustrates how the LOC compounds. If interest rates rise over the course of the loan, the LOC would, in time, outstrip the value of the house if housing values rise at a typical 3% or 4% annually.

Figure 10.1: Compounding growth of HECM LOC vs. HELOC

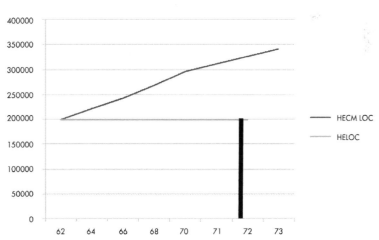

Combination

Homeowners may combine two or more configurations. For example, a borrower with a $225,000 initial credit capacity may take $50,000 in a lump sum, $500 a month on a seven-year term in order to avoid taking an early Social Security benefit, and leave the rest in a growing LOC.

A word on changing the distribution choice

Don't pay your reverse mortgage completely off! Check with the servicer to see what minimum balance is required to keep the loan in force. Having paid the set-up fees, you do not want to lose the remaining line of credit. You never know when you may need the money.

A fixed-rate HECM requires a full lump sum draw when the loan is consummated. This results in zero access to future draws. The payout options, however, are not locked in with adjustable-rate HECMs.

Most loan servicers will charge the loan balance a nominal fee ($25) to rearrange how an adjustable-rate HECM is distributed. It is possible, for example, to convert a tenure payment to an LOC and back. The calculation is based, in the background, on what the original Principal Limit (credit capacity) has grown to be, and the current age of the youngest participant. The original expected rate used at the loan's inception is applied to determine a conversion from the LOC to tenure payments.

For example, a client may start with tenure payments, and then decide to slow the housing consumption, and debt, by switching to an LOC. The payments will cease and whatever available credit is left flows into the LOC. The

LOC will grow monthly. Years later the client may want to resume monthly tenure payments. The current LOC, the original expected rate, and the age of the youngest eligible participant will determine the amount of those monthly payments.

The new tenure payment could be quite high due to advanced age and the large LOC from which the payment will fund it. This effect is accentuated if interest rates were low at loan inception (a bigger credit limit) but rose to a higher rate over the years. These phenomena would cause accelerated growth on a larger initial LOC, resulting in a higher payment.

CASE STUDY: REVOLVING LINE OF CREDIT

Curtis Cloke, CLTC, LUTCF, RICP, CEO and founder of Thrive University, and member of the Funding Longevity Task Force, helped a client rearrange and repurpose their reverse mortgage. When they began the plan in 2011, they were running out of money. They were expecting to inherit $200,000 when a parent died. Not wishing the parent to die prematurely, they put a HECM in place to replace their current mortgage. Not having that payment allowed them to relax and enjoy their retirement. When the inheritance did arrive, they paid down their HECM loan balance (to just $100) and watched their LOC compound at roughly 5%. After a few months they decided to take $1,000 a month to ease meeting their expenses. Even with those monthly draws, the LOC is growing, and the couple expects to have a large benefit to draw on for many years to come.

Conclusion

The HECM program is flexible and, as long as the credit capacity is not exhausted, it allows the borrower to mix and match different payment options. Over the life of the loan the homeowner can adjust draw patterns to reflect current needs. More money either left in or returned to the line of credit results in greater equity access for future needs, especially if interest rates rise. It is best to set up a reverse mortgage while interest rates are low. The initial available credit will be at its highest, and future growth in the LOC will benefit from rising interest rates over time.

ELEVEN

What Professor Wade Pfau Discovered About Reverse Mortgages

We are fortunate that Dr. Wade Pfau joined the Funding Longevity Task Force and took such an interest in the housing asset that he has written the definitive book on reverse mortgages, *Reverse Mortgages: How to Use Reverse Mortgages to Secure Your Retirement*. (Be sure you use the second edition.) Dr. Pfau begins by explaining retirement risks such as longevity, spending shocks, cognitive decline, and the enhanced sensitivity to investment returns the retiree faces due to market volatility, interest-rate spikes, and credit limits (especially for those without labor income). He counsels the reader to follow his Retirement-Researcher Manifesto, including:

- Playing the long game

- Using reasonable, not inflated assumptions on what the retirement portfolio will earn

- Integrating insurance solutions with investment solutions

- Assessing all household assets and liabilities and matching them to ongoing spending needs

Yup, you guessed it, Dr. Pfau believes that the home can be a retirement asset. He is aware, also, that a traditional mortgage in retirement can dangerously increase the retiree's fixed expenses. It's just common sense that the fewer the number of fixed obligations in the monthly budget, the better the retiree is able to withstand a temporary drop in the retirement portfolio's value. For this reason, Dr. Pfau compared a retirement plan that entails monthly mortgage payments to a plan that used a reverse mortgage to replace that traditional mortgage. Not stopping there, Dr. Pfau then wondered what would happen if the retiree made voluntary payments on a HECM reverse mortgage, thus increasing the HECM line of credit. Harkening back to the original research by Dr. Sacks (Chapters 9 and 10), Dr. Pfau then tested whether it made sense to cease making those payments in years when the portfolio experienced negative returns—the Coordinated Strategy.

"Refinancing the mortgage with a HECM allows for a noticeable improvement in success rates relative to strategies that continue with payments" to make monthly mortgage payments from the portfolio. "Success rates are improved even further" by replacing the mortgage with a HECM but making voluntary payments to build up the HECM LOC. This large LOC can act as a backstop later in retirement, if needed.

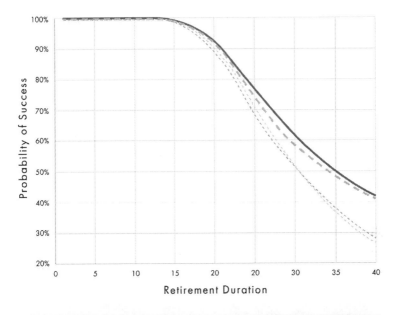

Figure 11.1: Refinance Mortgage with HECM: Probability of success for a 4% post-tax initial withdrawal rate, $1 million portfolio, $541,833 home value, 25% marginal tax rate

Dr. Pfau then evaluated the HECM for Purchase option to see if using the proceeds from the HECM to finance the new home would achieve similar results to replacing a mortgage with a HECM in a home the retiree wishes to remain in.

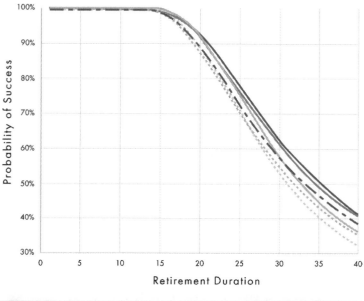

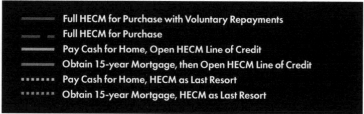

Figure 11.2: *HECM for Purchase compared to monthly mortgage payments or portfolio financing*

The best outcome is to use HECM for Purchase to cover as much of the home cost as allowed. Going forward, when the market provides positive returns, make a voluntary payment equal to the traditional mortgage payment but *skip these payments after down markets.* The HECM LOC will build up and can be used later in retirement if the portfolio depletes.

Social Security bridge

Dr. Pfau also provides guidance on a strategy to use a HECM as a bridge in order to defer Social Security benefits. It is well understood now that retirees should delay claiming their Social Security for as long as possible up to age seventy. Delayed Social Security benefits grow by 8% a year and max out at age seventy. For some people this delay is just not possible; they need the money now. In keeping with his mantra that you have to play the long game and plan for longevity, Dr. Pfau compared using a reverse mortgage to bridge the income needs while delaying claiming Social Security.

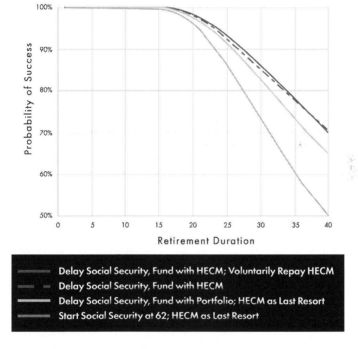

Figure 11.3: Comparison delaying Social Security using HECM as an income bridge

The two strategies supporting the highest success rates both involve delaying Social Security and funding the delay through distributions from a HECM rather than distributions from the investment portfolio. This affirms that even after accounting for the full retail costs of setting up a reverse mortgage, its ability to help reduce sequence risk for the portfolio by providing a way to delay Social Security without needing to take larger distributions from the portfolio provides greater net advantages.

Conclusion

Dr. Pfau reiterates that waiting to set up a HECM can be foolhardy for two reasons:

- The amount of credit available is more sensitive to interest rates than age

- Waiting causes the loss of compounding growth in the HECM line of credit

Dr. Pfau's book also provides a peek at legacy values when the HECM is used. I encourage you purchase a copy as well as to visit his website, where he has created a free, online reverse mortgage calculator.[1] The website provides expert, thoughtful advice on all aspects of retirement income planning.

Note

1   www.retirementresearcher.com.

TWELVE

Other Strategies For Using Housing Wealth In Retirement Planning

So, let's review the concepts that have driven interest in reverse mortgages among financial advisers. First, the dangers posed by a prolonged and/or early adverse sequence of returns can be mitigated by substituting draws from a HECM line of credit rather than taking draws from the portfolio when it is dangerously under-valued. We have seen that a goal in retirement should be to reduce fixed expenses in order to avoid mandatory draws on the portfolio. Replacing a traditional mortgage with a HECM or using a HECM for Purchase can reduce the need for both making monthly payments and drawing on the portfolio. We have seen also that making voluntary payments on the HECM and the HECM for Purchase builds up the LOC for later use if the portfolio depletes. And we have seen that the best outcome for the overall retirement security is established if those voluntary payments are stopped temporarily when the portfolio is under stress.

Having mastered these general concepts, we can move on to other HECM uses that advisers recommend.

Let's begin with Jamie Hopkins, Esq., LLM, CFP, ChFC, CLU, Director of Research at the Carson Group. Mr. Hopkins is perhaps the most vocal advocate for a change in how financial advisers approach the housing asset. In his book *Rewirement*, he states that retirees "need a new mantra when making housing decisions: cash flow, cash flow, cash flow. Cash flow is king in retirement. Without it you cannot meet your retirement income needs."

Professor Hopkins notes that using a reverse mortgage can provide three major benefits:

- Free up cash flow

- Restrict debt obligations

- Supplement retirement income

Would you pay extra for a loan that allows you to skip payments?

When speaking to groups about the fact that a reverse mortgage costs more than a regular mortgage, Mr. Hopkins asks the audience, "Would anybody in here pay extra for a mortgage that allows you to skip payments if you lose your job?" Of course, many people raise their hands in affirmation. He then states that in retirement, because you have no labor income, a drop in the value of your portfolio is like losing your job for a period of time. The reverse mortgage allows you to take a *payment holiday* anytime you want or even be on permanent payment holiday. His approach to retirement planning is approachable and entertaining—another good book to add to your retirement library.

Divorce in silver years: Realtors©, pay close attention!

A couple of years ago we started hearing from loan officers that divorce attorneys and financial planners had found a way to establish equity in housing in divorce. It turns out the Silver Divorce is widespread and growing. Often, the wife wants desperately to stay in the family home, and the children want her to as well, but there are not enough assets to allow the departing spouse to move to equivalent housing. This causes a sale of the legacy house which can be very unpleasant. We got together a little committee, and this is what we learned. If the couple has a property settlement agreement, a HECM can be put in place and all of the funds can be withdrawn as a lump sum. All of a sudden, we learned that divorce is considered an FHA mandatory obligation and not subject to initial distribution limits. There are two scenarios that work with the HECM.

In solution 1, a HECM on the marital home provides funds for the departing spouse's down payment on a new home. A Home-Purchase HECM pays the rest of the purchase price. There is no debt-service obligation for either spouse, and no forced sale of the marital home! In addition, the chances that both spouses retain homes of comparable value are enhanced.

In solution 2 the marital home is sold and proceeds divided. Each spouse uses their share to cover down payment on new home they desire, using a Home-Purchase HECM to pay the rest. There is no debt-service obligation for either spouse. Additionally, this solution may reduce or eliminate the need to take money from either spouse's portfolio while acquiring desirable housing for both.

Notice that the second scenario generates three sales.

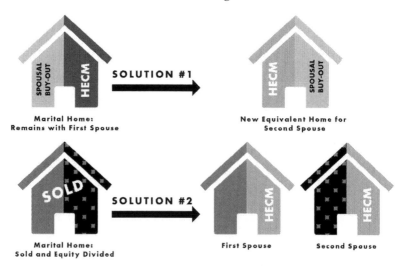

Figure 12.1: *HECM as divorce solution*

Tax equivalents

There is growing interest in the HECM by portfolio theorists and other academicians, in part because of tax considerations. When a client borrows money from the house via a HELOC, the draws from that loan are not treated as income for tax purposes. Likewise, proceeds from a HECM loan are not treated as income for tax purposes.

Therefore, drawing from the HECM LOC may have tax advantages over other forms of cash flow during retirement. In the *Journal of Financial Planning*, Gerald Wagner, PhD, noted in his paper "The 6% Solution":

> For example, a sixty-three-year-old borrower with $250,000 available for a payment plan could receive $1,449 each month from a HECM tenure plan; that is $17,387 per year, and because these are nontaxable loan advances, the payment's tax equivalent value is considerably higher. If the marginal federal bracket was 28.0%, and the borrower lived in California (10.3% tax rate), the tax equivalent value of these tenure advances would be $26,740.[1]

For this client, drawing home equity at the rate of $17,387 is the equivalent of having drawn $26,740 from his portfolio. Thomas C. B. Davison, MA, PhD, CFP®, discovered the same tax advantage in using home equity when compared to portfolio draws (private correspondence): "The way to figure out what you can spend is first to figure out what the tax is, then subtract that from the withdrawal, and spend what's left. If the tax rate is 33%, then the tax on $1.50 is $1.50 x 0.33, which is $0.49.5, leaving you $1.00 to spend after a bit of rounding. Or in fractions: the tax is (1/3) x $1.50 = $1.50/3, or 50 cents."

For every dollar spent in home equity, that is $1.50 not withdrawn from the portfolio.

Tax bracket creep

Others have noted that substituting draws from a reverse mortgage to avoid large draws from other assets may prevent triggering a higher tax rate. For example, Dr. Pfau wrote: "Proceeds from a reverse mortgage or from the cash value of life insurance could also be used in such a way to boost spending without increasing taxable income."[2]

Understanding how interest payments on HECM loans are deductible

People who plan to use their HECM as a revolving line of credit want to know how payments on the loan balance can qualify for mortgage interest deductions. Of course, mortgage interest is only deductible when *paid*. Reverse mortgages are treated the same way as traditional forward mortgages; mortgage interest is deductible, but only when paid, not just accrued. Because the HECM loan balance increases at not only the interest rate but the MIP rate as well, care must be taken to determine how much of the total amount owed is interest and hence can be deducted.

The ongoing 0.50% MIP is not considered interest, although it is part of the compounding rate. The actual interest charge is the sum of the variable component indexed to the Libor plus the unchanging lender's margin.

Acquisition debt versus consumption (home equity) debt

The 2017 Tax Cut and Jobs Act (TCAJA) changed how interest accrual on mortgages can be deducted. Although I am certainly not giving tax advice, I can state here that only interest that accumulates on "acquisition" debt qualifies. A HECM for Purchase is a home acquisition debt. Check with your accountant to determine whether or not your reverse mortgage qualifies as refinancing an original acquisition mortgage. If the HECM is used for or replaces debt used for significant home improvements, it is still considered acquisition debt. If your mortgages were undertaken for consumption, termed "home equity debt", interest is not deductible.

When interest is paid

If the borrower does not make payments on a mortgage until the loan ends, all the interest will be paid off as a lump sum, resulting in a large deduction in one year. The deduction may be larger than the taxable income in that year! It may be used on the estate tax return if the home is sold and the mortgage paid off after death.

The payment waterfall for purposes of deducting interest

As the monthly addition to the loan balance is both MIP and interest, not all of it will be deductible. Before a payment on the loan balance can be applied to the interest, the payment must be large enough to zero out the component of the loan that is allocated to MIP and servicing fees, if any. If you currently have a HECM reverse mortgage, then your payments are applied in the following order:

> first to that part of your loan balance representing mortgage insurance premiums, secondly to that part of your loan balance representing servicing fees, thirdly to that part of your loan balance representing interest charges, and finally to that part of your loan balance representing principal advances.

> The National Reverse Mortgage Lenders Association strongly advises that you confirm with your loan servicer the manner in which your partial prepayments will be applied to your specific account. (NRMLA, 2014)

A payment will at most be partially deductible. Any payment less than the currently accumulated MIP and servicing fees would not be deductible. Note that the interest component of the monthly compounding rate will be larger than the MIP and servicing fees—typically a much larger fraction, especially as interest rates rise. In the standby reverse mortgage scenario used by Salter et al., all the money borrowed in market downturns was paid back when markets recovered, so all the interest paid during that market downturn would be deductible.[3]

Tax bunching

In his blog Nerd's Eye View, Michael Kitces describes the new TCAJA categories limits for acquisition debt and home equity debt in his piece "Acquisition And Home Equity Mortgage Interest Tax Deductibility After TCJA":

> Under the Tax Cuts and Jobs Act of 2017 the debt limit on deductibility for acquisition indebtedness is reduced to just $750,000 (albeit grandfathered for existing mortgages under the old higher $1 million limit), and interest on home equity indebtedness is no longer deductible *at all* starting in 2018.[4]

Another Kitces blog describes timing of payments on the reverse mortgage aimed at overcoming the new high standard deduction.[5] Payments can be bunched in order to address itemizing deductions in years where enough off-setting income has been realized.

The lost tax deduction for estate planning

As a result of a conversation with loan officer Nick Maningas of Philadelphia, Dr. Barry H. Sacks investigated the effect of taking a deduction of the accumulated interest from a reverse mortgage to offset the income tax due from the borrower's heir(s) following the borrower's death:

> The use of the reverse mortgage results in accrued interest. Because the interest is accrued, but is not usually paid by the borrower, the borrower does not have an income tax deduction for that interest. The interest deduction seems to be lost. However, that deduction can be recovered by the borrower's beneficiary in the following way: 401(k) accounts and rollover IRAs are among the few assets, that, when left to beneficiaries, subject the beneficiaries to income tax. Some or all of that income tax can be eliminated by the use of the following simple technique:
>
> • Be sure that the decedent's home, which is subject to the reverse mortgage debt, goes **directly** to the same heir (or heirs) who is (or are) the beneficiary (or beneficiaries) of the decedent's 401(k) account or rollover IRA.
>
> • Be sure that the home becomes a "qualified residence" (as defined in the Internal Revenue Code) of the heir (or heirs) <u>before</u> it is sold. (The conventional approach to dealing with the assets would be to have the estate sell the

home and distribute the proceeds. The approach described is different from the conventional approach, and may need to be written into the client's will or trust).[6]

Tax-free way to fund other financial needs?

There are no restrictions on how HECM funds are used. It is possible to use tax-free HECM draws to fund existing insurance policies, or create new ones. Beneficiaries, of course, receive those life insurance proceeds tax-free.

Long-term care

Self-insure: Some advisers view the compounding growth in the HECM LOC as a way of self-insuring for long-term care. If the long-term care expense never materializes, the client has lost nothing by setting up the fund but has certainly hedged against the possibility that future health care needs could otherwise drain assets.

Keep policy in effect: For families that have a long-term care policy and other insurance benefits in effect, the cash flow provided by a reverse mortgage can help continue those protections.

Purchase LTC insurance: As a caution, clients considering using housing wealth to purchase LTC insurance are advised to make sure that the policy premiums can be sustained until the care is needed. In *Falling Short: The*

Coming Retirement Crisis, authors Charles D. Ellis, Alicia H. Munnell, and Andrew D. Eschtruth

strongly favor a catastrophic policy with premiums paid up front. This product would pay for benefits only after the individual has paid, for say, 12 months of nursing home care, or $80,000. This arrangement would change an unbounded black hole of expense into a known quantity. Moreover, the premium for this benefit would be relatively modest and could be paid in single lump sum at retirement so buyers need not worry about premium costs climbing as they age. The hope would be that once people understood the dimensions for their exposure to long-term care costs, they would feel more comfortable about spending their balances and tapping their home equity. Unfortunately, such a product does not currently exist in the United States.

Roth Conversion taxes and NUA

It may make sense to pay taxes on a lump sum of company stock and take advantage of net unrealized appreciation (NUA). Or if it makes sense to convert an account to a Roth IRA, it can be difficult to fund the tax bite from the portfolio. A reverse mortgage represents an alternative bucket of tax-free cash. Using money from the traditional IRA itself to pay the taxes would reduce the remaining IRA amount. For example, if the taxpayer is in the 30% tax bracket, and converts a $100,000 traditional IRA, paying the tax with money from the IRA, the remaining IRA amount, in the Roth IRA, will be $70,000. If instead the taxpayer uses a reverse mortgage credit line draw to pay the tax, there will be $100,000 in the Roth IRA. Growth in a Roth IRA is not taxable. I am not giving tax advice here, so be sure to consult your tax professional. In fact, a recent article in the *Wall Street Journal* quoted IRA expert Ed Slott warning that Roth Conversions can cause unintended repercussions.[7]

Defer Social Security by using the HECM as an income bridge

The media continue to highlight strategies on how to maximize Social Security benefits. Many people would like to defer taking benefits until age seventy because of the substantial increase in benefits earned with that delay.[8] The chart below demonstrates that a delay in taking benefits results in a much higher monthly payment.

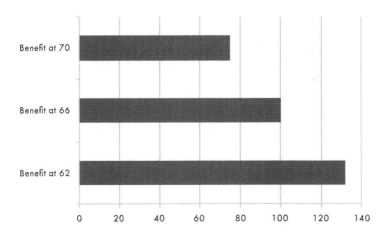

Figure 12.2: Social Security benefits by age, % full Social Security benefit

CASE STUDY

The problem with waiting until age seventy is giving up income in those years from sixty-two to seventy until qualifying for the maximum payout at seventy. Thomas C. B. Davison, MA, PhD, CFP® published a case study on his blog *http://www.toolsforretirementplanning.com*, in which the client uses home equity for income during many of the deferral years. The survival probability for the client's plan improved from 5% to 90%. This case illustrates how a homeowner could use a reverse mortgage to fund her needs for the first six years. Once the HECM funds are exhausted, she relies on her portfolio. But at age seventy, she is able to reduce her portfolio draws because she is getting the largest possible Social Security benefit. Interestingly, the reasons her plan showed such improvement in financial stability are not just related to getting a higher Social Security benefit at seventy:

- This client's reverse mortgage funded six+ years of spending.

- She had more assets to spend because she added $240,000 in home wealth to her $500,000 IRA.

- Taxes matter: This client was in the 33%+ tax bracket, state/federal combined. The reverse mortgage was tax-free, so every $1.00 draw has the spending power of $1.50 drawn from the IRA. In total, the $240,000 spent from her reverse mortgage was the equivalent of $360,000 of IRA funds.

Social Security starts at 62:
IRA Funds Remaining Income Gap

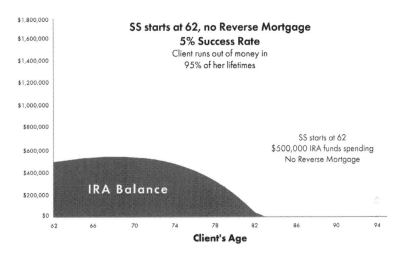

Delayed Social Security:
Reverse Mortgage Funds Income Gap

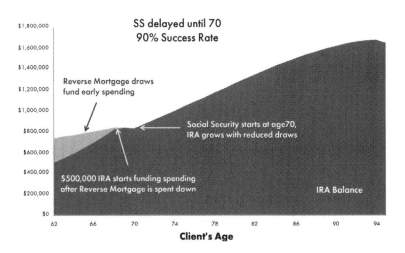

Figure 12.3: *Portfolio comparison using HECM to fund deferral years*

137

- The investment portfolio was untouched for an extra six years. Keeping the portfolio invested reduces chances that she will encounter a bad sequence of returns early in retirement.

- At age seventy, she enjoys the highest Social Security benefits possible, further reducing portfolio draws in her later years.

The HECM as a hedge against inflation

Dr. Jack Guttentag has been a vocal HECM proponent for years on his website.[9] Dr. Guttentag is a Professor Emeritus at the University of Pennsylvania Wharton School of Business. Never one to mince words, Dr. Guttentag states:

> The HECM reverse mortgage is one of the best engineered financial tools of our generation, designed to meet a wide spectrum of senior needs, from repairing the roof of their home, to paying for their grandchildren's education, to meeting expected and unexpected contingencies. Yet the program elicits negative reactions from large segments of the media, whose distorted descriptions of the HECM program are scaring off millions of seniors whose lives could be enriched by it.

He recommends that retirees establish a HECM line of credit early enough to enjoy compounding growth for many years:

The use of the HECM reverse mortgage program as a type of insurance policy employs the credit line feature of the program. The senior uses her borrowing power to draw the largest line available, and lets the line sit unused until she needs it. The longer the senior lives, the longer the credit line sits unused, and the larger it becomes. While her financial assets are gradually being depleted, her credit line is getting larger. She draws on the line if she needs the money, otherwise the equity in her house will pass to her estate.

Why the urgency? The size of the initial HECM credit lines that can be drawn are inversely related to interest rates, while the growth rate of existing unused lines is directly related to rates. Hence, a senior with a specified amount of equity gets the maximum insurance coverage by taking out the HECM while interest rates are still low, and letting it sit unused as rates rise in the future.

Table 12.1: *Higher interest rates provide a greater line of credit over time*

Initial Line	Effective Rate (Growth in LOC)	Unused Line of Credit at 10 Years
$97,800	5%	$177,700
$97,800	6%	$195,300
$97,800	7%	$214,600
$97,800	8%	$235,600

In this case, for example, the client begins with a $97,800 HECM LOC. If left untouched for ten years, technically her line of credit would have grown to $195,300 if the growth rate were 6%.[10]

Medicare gap: Watch your MAGI

Retirement healthcare adviser Rob Klein notes:

> [It] is important to pay attention to modified adjusted gross income [MAGI] when you are enrolled in Medicare. Earning one dollar too much over $85,000 or $170,000 (single/married filing jointly), is enough to buy you a 40% premium surcharge to your Medicare Part B and a surcharge to your Part D prescription drug plan. This is called the income related monthly adjusted amount or IRMAA. If you are receiving Social Security, Part B and IRMAA surcharges to Parts B and D must be deducted from your benefit. Given that Medicare is expected to inflate annually around 5% to 7% and Social Security is not expected to have a cost of living adjustment (COLA) increase more than 2.8% (some years it's a small amount or there is none), this will be very expensive over time. It is important you and your financial advisers understand which income Medicare considers income and which is does not. Home equity is not considered income by Medicare.

The HECM as a hedge against declining home values

Dr. Pfau published an article in *Advisor Perspectives* demonstrating that establishing a HECM line of credit early provides a hedge against home values dropping:

> With the current HECM rules, those living in their homes long enough could reap a large windfall when the line of credit exceeds the home's value. This potential windfall is amplified by today's low interest rates. Even if the value of the home declines, the line of credit will continue to grow without regard for the home's subsequent value.

Because the HECM is a non-recourse loan, there is no restriction from drawing down the LOC even if its value is greater than the current value of the house.

CASE STUDY

We know of a borrower who set her LOC during the housing bubble when her home value was very high. When she developed Alzheimer's and had to move during the Great Recession, her home value had dropped precipitously. But her LOC was still going strong and was, in fact, greater in value than her home. She took a lump sum draw from her LOC, a perfectly admissible action, and she was not liable for the gap between her loan balance and the amount her home brought at sale.

Caution: The ruthless option[11]

Before the changes of October 2, 2017 to the Principal Limit factors, some lenders were marketing the LOC as a "ruthless option." They encouraged advisers to put their clients in a HECM LOC with the highest possible interest rate margin. Loans with high interest rate margins are lucrative when sold on the secondary market and lenders sweetened the pot by offering lender credits to the homeowner to cover closing costs. At the time the mortgage insurance upfront fee (MIP) was reduced for low utilization loans. The lenders were counting on the borrower making future draws at a high interest rate even though they were *marketing* the LOC as a buy-and-hold strategy. Lender amortization schedules were produced showing the LOC growing into the millions of dollars because of the high margin. This was a deliberate attempt to game the non-recourse feature and leave the taxpayer holding the bill for paying out on an enormous LOC against a home value that would not cover the debt. Worse yet, since the ruthless option purported to depend on a very low loan balance for many years, the contribution over time to the FHA mortgage insurance (MIP) would be close to nil. This is a case of rich people not doing their part if there ever was one.

The Funding Longevity Task Force took a stand against this marketing ploy. To deliberately use the taxpayer backstop in this way is particularly cynical. The Task Force read the Code of Federal Regulations carefully and concluded that the amortization schedules purporting that the HECM LOC grows unbridled were wrong. The Code states that

HECM distributions are limited to a maximum mortgage amount (150% of the Maximum Claim Amount, usually the home value). Although there is language in the Code about loan modifications, nowhere does it state that a borrower has a right to a loan modification for a grossly inflated LOC amount. There are no guidelines about a new home appraisal to support a loan modification to a new mortgage amount in later years of the mortgage. Nor are there provisions for what a new maximum mortgage amount requirement would be if a borrower extracted a huge LOC in the millions of dollars and started incurring interest charges on it.

Luckily the October 2, 2017 changes have mostly eradicated the ruthless option as a marketing scheme. The Principal Limit floor is lower, which means that lenders are reducing interest rate margins in order to provide the highest possible amount of initial benefit. There is less profit in the loans so less incentive for the lender to extend closing cost credits. Also, the October 2, 2017 changes require that every HECM loan adequately fund the mortgage insurance, whether or not the borrower uses his or her money today or twenty years in the future. Again, these increased upfront costs have reduced the lender enthusiasm for advertising the HECM as a zero-cost loan.

Home care

Nursing home stays in the US have declined over the years, and no wonder. Have you ever known anyone to raise a hand and say, "Take me to a nursing home, please"?

Retirees have a strong desire to age at home. An Age Wave/ Merrill Lynch survey in 2015 entitled *Home in Retirement: More Freedom, New Choices* provides context for this. The desire to stay at home is so strong that retirees are spending billions of dollars a year on improving their homes. The HGTV effect for retirees often includes opening up the kitchen into a great room to accommodate gatherings with children and grandchildren, putting a bedroom and bathroom on the bottom floor, and working with universal design principles for wheelchair functionality. For those who move, downsizing does not seem to be the default choice. In fact, when retirees move they often move to a larger home!

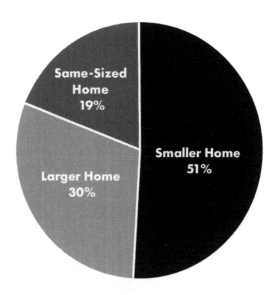

Base: Age 50+ retirees who have moved since retiring

Figure 12.4: *Home size choice for retirees who have moved home in retirement: more freedom, new choices*

Retirees overwhelmingly prefer home to anywhere else. The Home Care Association of America indicates that nine out of ten Americans want to stay at home as long as possible. And certainly a reverse mortgage can help fund that preference. There is real harmony in the idea that the home will provide the means for staying in the home. Home care seems to be cost-efficient to the taxpayer, as well. According to the Association, home caregivers can help save $25 billion in hospital costs by managing senior needs within the home, which, of course, would represent less of a drain on Medicare and Medicaid. For the children who are often sandwiched between taking care of their parents and their own children, the HCAOA cites the deleterious effects on them in the workplace:

"More than 40 million American workers are caring for loved ones and relatives over age 65. Six in 10 are balancing their caregiving responsibilities with full- or part-time jobs. Caring for a loved one while juggling demands at work can be time-consuming and emotionally draining. The stress and distractions of caregiving can reduce worker productivity and put a strain on mental and physical health, which comes at a cost to employers. Home care eases this responsibility and enables workers to remain productive while on the job."[12]

Funding for real estate taxes with the HECM LESA

Dr. Pfau taught us that having fewer fixed expenses in retirement allows the retiree to navigate adverse markets more easily because there is less mandatory drain on the portfolio. But every homeowner has a real estate tax burden.

If you have not yet explored what your town or county allows in tax deferrals and reductions for seniors, stop here and do it now!

But for most people, taxes are as inevitable as death, or so said Benjamin Franklin. There is a way to escrow your tax and insurance obligations with a reverse mortgage. This gives many homeowners tremendous peace of mind knowing that the lender will make those payments. If this appeals to you, ask for a LESA with your HECM. The LESA is a life-expectancy set-aside deducted from your overall benefit as an escrow for the express purpose of funding your tax and insurance (including flood if required) needs based on your life expectancy and inflation. As Joe Ferraro, a HECM expert in Connecticut, explains:

> A LESA allows homeowners to manage their burden similar to the escrow arrangement they might have had with a forward mortgage for thirty or so years. As a result, there is every reason to believe they would rather have the lender set this equity aside and take on the obligation of making those tax and insurance

payments. In addition, the total amount needed based on the LESA math formula (FV) can be reduced (PV) when the LOC growth factor (similar to an IRR) is applied. This results in less funds being deducted from the Principal Limit for the LESA compared to what would be the borrower's out-of-pocket payment obligation.

Table 12.2: LESA calculation

First Year Annual Taxes	$5,800.00
First Year Annual Insurance	$780.00
Total First Year T & I	$6,580.00
Annual First Year T & I times 1.2 Inflation Factor	$7,896.00
Times Life Expectancy of Youngest Borrower Minus One Year	9
Total 2nd Year – 12th Year Set-Aside Needed	$71,064.00
Total Amount Needed for Set-Aside (including 1st year drawn at closing)	$85,549.00
Discounted Set-Aside Required with LOC Growth Factor (5.37%)	$61,264.80
Amount Saved with LOC Growth Applied to Present Value Versus	$9,799.20

Courtesy of Joe Ferraro

Conclusion

It is unrealistic and uninformed to ignore the housing asset in retirement. The last-resort strategy was never subjected to any thoughtful or quantitative analysis; the financial world just blindly accepted that a reverse mortgage "should" only be used when all other assets were exhausted. When this approach was subjected to the bright light of mathematics, there was no reason to continue advocating a "wait-and-pray" approach. This is especially true now that academicians fully understand how the HECM line of credit compounds over the course of retirement. Recent research treats the HECM as an alternative asset that can be used in concert with other sources of income, often with a synergistic effect.

Notes

1   Wagner, Gerald C. "The 6.0 Percent Rule." *Journal of Financial Planning* 26/12 (2013), 46.

2   http://blogs.wsj.com/experts/2015/03/19/how-to-increase-your-after-tax-wealth-in-retirement/.

3   Thomas C. B. Davison, MA, PhD, CFP®, www.toolsforretirementplanning.com.

4   www.kitces.com/blog/tcja-home-mortgage-interest-tax-deduction-for-acquisition-indebtedness-vs-home-equity-heloc.

5   www.kitces.com/blog/hecm-reverse-mortgage-interest-deduction-insurance-premiums-and-real-estate-taxes/.

6   Sacks, Barry H., Nicholas Maningas, Sr., Stephen R. Sacks, and Francis Vitagliano, "Recovering a Lost Deduction", *Journal of Taxation*, 124/4 (2016), 157–69.

7   https://www.wsj.com/articles/when-to-ignore-the-crowd-and-shun-a-roth-ira-1534498202.

8   For an overview of Social Security claiming strategies, see Mary Beth Franklin at: http://www.investmentnews.com/section/retirement2.

9   http://www.mtgprofessor.com.

10 http://mtgprofessor.com/A%20-%20Reverse%20Mortgages/avoid_outliving_your_money_by_taking_a_HECM_reverse_mortgage_now.html.

11 Thanks to Tom Davidoff, Associate Professor, Sauder School of Business, University of British Columbia.

12 www.hcaoa.org/file.aspx?DocumentId=134.

THIRTEEN

The Cash-Poor Myth

You may have thought that reverse mortgages are only for people who are broke. Because retirement researchers have actually quantified how the housing asset can contribute to retirement security for those with assets other than their home, more people than ever before can benefit from the wealth that they have built up in their homes. As we have noted, the HECM has changed significantly over time. Accordingly, the typical reverse mortgage borrower looks very different than those in the past. Although the National Reverse Mortgage Lenders Association reports that there is over $6 *trillion* of home equity owned by Americans aged sixty-two and older, one "in four Medicare recipients has less than $12,250 in home equity," according to a new report by the Kaiser Family Foundation, a healthcare non-profit.

Kaiser's calculations also show that the distribution of home equity among older Americans is—like the distribution of income and financial assets—top heavy. While 5%

of Medicare beneficiaries in 2013 had more than $398,500 in home equity, half have less than $66,700. According to Kaiser's projections, that gap will widen in the future: "By 2030, those whose home equity places them in the top 5% will see that equity grow more than 40%, but it will rise less than 10% for those with mid-level—or median—amounts of equity."[1]

The sad truth is that reverse mortgages will not substantially help the homeowners with few financial resources. Unfortunately, these folks had been targeted inappropriately in the past. Homeowners who could not, or would not, meet their tax and insurance obligations were encouraged to consume all of their reverse mortgage credit in one huge draw.

Actually, the full-draw choice was the only available option for many of these clients. Thousands of older Americans had been caught up in the frenzied housing bubble and had already compromised their equity with subprime, high-LTV, cash-out loans. In order to participate in a reverse mortgage, they had no choice but to take a full lump sum draw to replace their high-LTV existing loans with a HECM. When these borrowers failed to meet their tax and insurance obligations, foreclosure was the only option.

In the meantime, housing values collapsed. The insurance fund at the FHA was stressed by having to make good on underwater loans. With his typically blunt style, in his 2015 article entitled "After March 2, Reverse Mortgage Borrowers Will Have to Prove They Are Not Deadbeats,"

Dr. Jack Guttentag writes:

> One of the attractive features of the HECM
> reverse mortgage has been that there are no
> income or credit requirements. All homeowners
> sixty-two and older who live in their homes
> without a mortgage have been eligible, and those
> with mortgages may also be eligible if the balance
> is not too large. But all that will change when a
> series of drastic new FHA rules come into play.
>
> The precipitating factor underlying the new
> rules is the marked rise that has occurred in
> recent years in property tax defaults by HECM
> borrowers. While such borrowers are violating
> their obligations under the reverse mortgage
> contract, and are thereby subject to foreclosure
> and eviction, FHA has been understandably
> reluctant to allow elderly homeowners to be
> thrown into the street. Instead, FHA has elected
> to impose income and credit requirements on
> future applicants. The purpose is to assure that
> henceforth borrowers will have both the capacity
> and the willingness to pay their property taxes
> and homeowners insurance.[2]

Always mindful of the ultimate bequest to heirs, Michael
Kitces, MSFS, MTAX, CFP®, CLU, ChFC, RHU, REBC,
CASL does point out:

> In essence, the intention of the new rules is to
> shift reverse mortgages from being used as a last

resort, to being used more proactively and earlier in the retirement process as a part of a coherent strategy; in other words, as a part of a more comprehensive financial planning approach.[3]

No evidence for the last-resort strategy

Despite the fact that newspapers continue to recommend a reverse mortgage as a "last resort," there is not a shred of evidence to support this statement. If you are planning on establishing a reverse mortgage only if all of your assets and your cash flow are totally depleted, that will be a pretty big hole to climb out of. Why not coordinate your home asset with your others in order to assure the most efficient use of what you have saved for your retirement? Taking on a reverse mortgage does not mean you have to spend it. But it sure is nice knowing it is there.

Coordinated versus Uncoordinated Approach

Toney Sebra, a reverse mortgage expert in California is concerned about financial advisers who are ill-informed on the powerful research supporting the early integration of the housing asset in retirement. Moreover, those advisers who do embrace the new ways of looking at reverse mortgages are often challenged by overcoming the entrenched stigma of reverse mortgages when they introduce them to their clients. He advises financial advisers, with just a note of exasperation, to ask their clients if they would prefer "a coordinated or an uncoordinated" retirement strategy! "The old methodology of financial planning is an uncoordinated approach whereby only the financial assets are considered to support the retirement picture... In the coordinated strategy both the financial assets and housing wealth are combined to strengthen, secure and improve overall retirement outcomes."

Exit strategy

A borrower who is using a reverse mortgage as a discretionary tool may want to consider an exit strategy should interest rates rise substantially. This could involve electing to make payments during high-interest-rate years in order to keep the loan balance low. Or it could mean paying the balance down. Don't forget that any payments result in a line of credit increase that will be there for possible future use. Generally, it does not make sense to pay off a reverse mortgage completely, although there are no prepayment penalties. A low balance of just $100 is all it takes to keep the mortgage in force and the LOC growing. The costs of maintaining such a low balance is *de minimis*, yet the utility of having rapid access to the growing LOC could be significant. As Jeff Brown of *Main Street* noted:

> Imagine having a retirement safety net that cost nothing to maintain and actually grew as you aged rather than getting smaller. How would that affect other parts of your financial plan?

Conclusion

Past events highlight how important it is to consume housing wealth prudently and with an eye to future needs. If staying in the home will stretch a homeowner's ability to meet tax, insurance, and maintenance obligations, the HECM is not an appropriate choice. The evolution of the HECM, much of which has been a result of changes adopted by HUD to protect the FHA fund, means that the likely beneficiaries are now middle- to upper-middle-class households. In restructuring how the loan proceeds, HUD has returned the HECM to Congress' original intent. The loan exists to help homeowners mobilize home equity throughout the distribution phase, to help fund a safe, more financially secure retirement. Investigators in the field describe today's ideal client as having invested assets somewhere in the range of $100,000 to $2 million *and* a house.

Notes

1   http://squaredawayblog.bc.edu/squared-away/1-in-4-seniors-have-little-home-equity/.

2   www.mtgprofessor.com/A%20-%20Reverse%20Mortgages/new_income_and_credit_requirements_for_HECM_borrowers.html.

3   www.kitces.com/blog/will-new-reverse-mortgage-changes-make-them-a-better-financial-planning-tool/.

FOURTEEN

When A Financial Adviser Will Not/Cannot Discuss The Housing Asset

As Americans move into retirement, they want to feel confident that their nest eggs will last as long as they do. At the same time, they don't want to live on such a strict budget that they cannot enjoy life. Many Americans rely on financial advisers of various stripes to guide them through the saving stage into the spending stage.

Few planners have had formal training on either reverse mortgages or the protective role that housing wealth can play in volatile markets. This is beginning to change somewhat. The American College of Financial Services, for example, offers a designation, the Retirement Income Certified Professional (RICP®), which provides advisers with a comprehensive view of retirement income planning. Part of that curriculum addresses housing and housing wealth, including reverse mortgage mechanics and strategies. According to the RICP® program director, David Littell, JD, ChFC®, CFP®:

> the research is clearly showing that reverse
> mortgages, if used properly, can increase
> sustainability of retirement income and total wealth.
> It would be a disservice to financial advisors and
> their clients not to include this in our curriculum.

Unfortunately, if a client mentions a reverse mortgage to the typical financial adviser, his questions are likely to be dismissed. Beware: The more general and vague the reasons offered for not discussing a reverse mortgage, the more likely the adviser has not mastered either the changes in reverse mortgages, the studies supporting housing wealth inclusion in retirement plans, or both. Or even more unfortunately he may want to discuss this with you, but his compliance department forbids it!

Fined for helping a client with a reverse mortgage

Don't laugh, as this actually happened. An adviser in Kalamazoo arranged for a client's sister-in-law to talk to a reverse mortgage originator. The woman is an ex-schoolteacher with no children. Certainly, she was an appropriate candidate for a reverse mortgage discussion. But the adviser's compliance department surveilled his email account and saw that he was in contact with a reverse mortgage lender. What did they do? They fined him $350!

Clients may be intimidated when the adviser scoffs at a request for information on a reverse mortgage. Many advisers may dismiss the conversation by making statements like "You don't want one of those," "They are too expensive," "I can't talk to you about that or I will get in trouble," or the all-time misinformed but common mistake, "You don't want to give your house to the bank."

If an adviser states that homeowners should wait to set up a HECM because they will receive more money when they are older, this is incorrect advice for three reasons:

Reason # 1

Although at any particular point in time an older borrower is eligible for more money than a younger one, the credit allowed (Principal Limit) is much more sensitive to prevailing interest rates than to age.

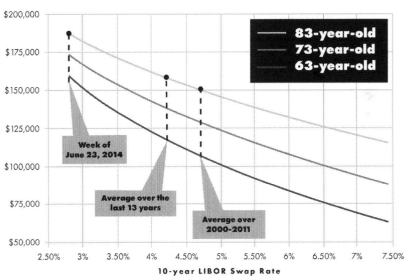

Figure 14.1: HECM benefits more sensitive to interest rates than homeowner age

Borrowers of different ages will be impacted by rising rates. If the ten-year swap rate goes up to its historic averages, benefits will be greatly reduced. (Chart and explanation courtesy of Gerald Wagner, PhD, President of Ibis Software.)

Reason #2

If the homeowner waits, he or she will miss the compounding growth in the line of credit that could fund the later years of retirement.

Reason #3

There is a real danger that the HECM as we know it today may not even exist twenty or thirty years from now. Public policy risk is real, as we have seen with abrupt changes in Social Security. We also do not know what housing values will be when the client needs liquidity, nor do we know what the interest rates will be in the future.

We *do* know that a HECM line of credit set up today will compound in borrowing power and be available until the homeowner exits the home permanently even decades in the future.

The folly of wait-and-see

Why such resistance in the financial services sector? Often advisers are unaware of what is changing because their initial training did not include housing wealth. Many advisers adhere to what they learned twenty or thirty years ago: If you go broke, *then* it's appropriate to take out a reverse mortgage. That advice reflects a passive wait-and-see (or pray!) attitude. It also reflects the emotional tie that many people have for burning the mortgage when they retire, and therefore being free of debt payments. This attitude became ingrained long before reverse mortgages were available to the general public, and long before the general public switched from employer-provided defined benefit pensions to 401(k) accounts that retirees had to manage themselves throughout retirement. People cling to this advice despite the fact that, as Drs. Sacks, Salter, Guttentag, and Pfau have demonstrated, relying on a reverse mortgage as a last resort results in the worst outcome. The notion that coordinating housing wealth in the plan may prevent portfolio exhaustion has not penetrated the financial planning community.

FINRA

Some advisers will insist that the Financial Industry Regulatory Authority (FINRA), the self-regulatory entity policing broker-dealer advisers, prohibits reverse mortgage lending. In fact, for some time, FINRA did recommend that reverse mortgages only be used as a last resort. Dr. Sacks challenged FINRA by establishing that this is a mathematically incorrect statement. Ultimately FINRA did alter its language in October 2013:

> FINRA is issuing this Alert to urge homeowners thinking about reverse mortgages to make informed decisions and carefully weigh all of their options before proceeding. And, if you do

decide a reverse mortgage is right for you, be sure to make prudent use of your loan.[1]

So back to compliance: An adviser understandably may avoid discussing housing wealth because his or her broker-dealer compliance officer forbids it. It is not clear why compliance officers would want to avoid aiding clients in preserving portfolio value. Some certainly fear that rogue advisers would inappropriately encourage clients to tap home equity in order to sell the client more securities. Doing so may subject the retired client to greater risk because the securities could lose value, which both is and should be prohibited.

What these broker-dealer compliance officers fail to understand is that current research does not suggest using housing wealth to purchase new securities, but rather advocates using housing wealth to protect against having to sell *existing* securities when their values are low.

Financial planning software deficiencies

To a certain extent, advisers are handicapped because their planning software will not provide a plan that incorporates housing wealth. Most advisers rely on financial planning software provided by their firms to prepare possible retirement scenarios for their clients. Unfortunately, most software vendors do not provide asset projections that can evaluate a plan with and without incorporating housing wealth. The retiree who pays for a personalized, colorful financial plan produced by planner software, in effect, is getting only one side of the story. Without a review of his or her housing wealth, the client cannot decide whether or not taking a reverse mortgage is suitable for his or her needs.

Paying for advice

American retirees pay for advice either through fees or commissions or both. The cost is not insignificant. To place this cost in perspective, a client with a starting portfolio of $1 million may pay an adviser a 1% assets-under-management fee, or $10,000 the first year. That is $10,000 subtracted from the portfolio that will not be available to fund retirement years.[2]

To stay roughly on budget, this client could draw 4% of the portfolio the first year, or $40,000. The second year in retirement, the client would pay the adviser another 1% of the remaining AUM (assets under management). Advice comes at a cost, and advisers are obligated to provide varying standards of care.[3]

The point here is not that people do not benefit from financial planning advice, but that they are entitled to accurate information and *informed advice* about whether or not their housing wealth can aid cash flow survival. At the very least, an adviser who confers with clients on the suitability of possibly including the housing wealth asset in a retirement plan provides more complete assistance than an adviser who is prohibited from discussing a reverse mortgage.

Ignoring cash flow in retirement advice

Jamie Hopkins frequently addresses financial advisers. Both a lawyer and an expert in retirement income planning, Hopkins is aware of litigation trends threatening financial services firms. He warns that ignoring cash flow advice is a dangerous direction to take in advising clients. He cites litigation in the life settlement arena as a possible precedent and warns his audiences not to ignore assets that contribute to cash flow.

Preserving assets under management

That some financial services firms reject learning how reverse mortgages work is even more perplexing when considering that AUM is so important to fee generation, both at the retail and the mutual fund levels. The *Wall Street Journal* reported in June of 2015 that 401(k) withdrawals by Boomers exceeded contributions, which will have an effect on large money managers. Dr. Sacks provides perspective:

> Suppose a retiree at age sixty-five has a portfolio worth $1 million. If that retiree decides to draw more than the SafeMax amount, and opts to use the Coordinated Strategy to manage his cash flow, clearly the mutual fund or other portfolio manager will retain more of the securities under management, for a longer time, than it would if the retiree were to use the Last Resort strategy. However, the mean of the difference between the mutual funds earnings over the thirty-year

period, under the Coordinated Strategy and the Last Resort strategy, discounted to present value at a 5% discount rate, for the $1 million portfolio (with a home value of greater than $600,000) turns out to be about $50,000. Carrying that analysis into the future, as the rest of the baby-boomer generation comes into retirement, it seems reasonable to conclude that at least another $50 million of increased fees should be realized. (Private correspondence.)

Who doesn't need a backup plan for a secure retirement?[4]

Professionals thinking deeply about the challenges Baby Boomers face in funding their own retirements inevitably alight on housing wealth. Michael Kitces, MSFS, MTAX, CFP®, CLU, ChFC, RHU, REBC, CASL, has noted that a standard mortgage requiring repayment could be counter-productive if the goal is to improve cash flow. By having to make payments each month, clients *deleverage* what they wanted to leverage in the first place. In comparison, a reverse mortgage leverages the housing asset to produce cash flow which may accomplish the client's goal more efficiently.

There simply is no way to know what the future holds. Establishing a well-priced emergency fund could be a wise strategy for just about anybody. Can the HECM be a life-boat? Better to think of the HECM, as my friend Shannon Hicks does, as the ultimate shock absorber. Not surprisingly, research by Stephanie Moulton, PhD, Associate

Professor, John Glenn College of Public Affairs at Ohio State University confirmed that many HECM clients in the past used it as an emergency fund following a credit shock.[5] Most people treat their home asset with the same respect they treat their other resources. What is missing is the understanding of why setting up a growing HECM line of credit *early* transforms an illiquid, indivisible asset into a powerful financial planning device of extraordinary power and versatility.

How can an adviser change the compliance prohibition?

The first step is to understand that FINRA does not prohibit a reverse mortgage discussion, nor does Errors and Omissions insurance. Curtis Cloke, CLTC, LUTCF, RICP points out a common misunderstanding in an interview:

> Another point I want to make is that there's also a perception held by financial planners and broker/dealers that their E&O (Errors and Omissions) insurance coverage prohibits them from providing financial advice about reverse mortgages. This is simply not true. The policy says they can't sell reverse mortgages, but there's nothing that says we can't advise on reverse mortgages. That's a key distinction, but it's the first objection you get from advisers. In my dealings with broker/dealers I realized that their compliance staff have their own beliefs and biases too.
>
> What's significant is that these compliance people are authorized by FINRA to avow or disavow

certain things from being discussed between a consumer and investment adviser, based solely on their approval. Many times, their own personal biases naturally and subliminally come into play. This is what I learned when I spoke to them about reverse mortgages. Keep in mind, you will never get a broker/dealer to approve a financial adviser to tell a client that they should, or should not, get a reverse mortgage.

Rather, there are certain things that advisers need to know and understand about financial tools and how they work. When they see a fact pattern emerging with a client, they will know enough to say "I don't sell reverse mortgages, and I can't tell you specifically how they work from company to company, but I see a fact pattern that tells me you should educate yourself about a possible reverse mortgage and seek out at least three different experts to get that level of detail."

Firm study group

Our Funding Longevity Task Force works with financial services firms to help them overcome these prohibitions. Sometimes it has taken a group of high-performing advisers within the firm to approach the compliance department together and ask to create a study group. This approach will often include legal, marketing, and the investment side of the house. A couple of other considerations that have fueled a change in compliance prohibitions are:

- The firm already allows advice on strategic mortgage refinancing and HELOCs.

- The firm allows directing clients to other professionals like estate lawyers, and CPAs, so why not a hand-off to a housing wealth expert?

After careful examination of the research, the conclusion is obvious: There is more risk in avoiding the housing asset than in providing access to that information.

Although convincing financial services firms to change has been slow, the reverse mortgage industry was elated when recently the prestigious Mutual of Omaha Bank acquired a reverse mortgage company, Retirement Funding Solutions.

Standard of care

I have danced around the entire notion of duty of care. It is absolutely not my role to tell an adviser what his or her responsibilities to his or her clients are. Oceans of ink and millions of dollars have been spent in either support or distain for the recently vacated Department of Labor Fiduciary Rule. Most recently, this concept of suitable advice is in the hands of the SEC in its proposed Reg Best Interest.[6] The regulation prohibits placing a firm's financial interests ahead of the interests of a customer in making investment recommendations or in securities transactions. Whether or not this rule encompasses the obligation to include housing wealth considerations in those discussions is an interesting question.

Conclusion

Sadly, many in the financial services community may know less about reverse mortgages than those who watch late night television. No doubt these omnipresent reverse mortgage infomercials have contributed to the product's bad reputation. Advisers are well aware of the possible shocks looming in retirement and are doing their best to help you withstand the future unknowns. If your financial adviser is uninformed or prevented from discussing the newly structured HECM and its costs, this should not dissuade you from having a conversation about a *possible* role the house can play in retirement. After all, you are paying for the advice.

Notes

1   http://www.finra.org/investors/alerts/reverse-mortgages-avoiding-reversal-fortune.

2   A future value calculator at dinkytown.net values the loss of this $10,000 over a thirty-year retirement at $57,444 at a 6% annual rate of return.

3   For a discussion about the differences between "fiduciary" versus "suitability" standards of advice, see https://www.thebalance.com/difference-between-fiduciary-and-suitability-4010117.

4   http://mandelman.ml-implode.com/2014/01/who-doesnt-need-a-back-up-plan-for-a-secure-retirement/.

5   https://u.osu.edu/aipstudyw2/.

6   www.sec.gov/rules/proposed/2018/34-83063.pdf.

FIFTEEN

Finding An Ethical Lender And Getting The Best Price?

As in any profession, there are scoundrels in reverse mortgage lending. It is important to find a reputable lender. Few people realize that once they engage with a lender, they can negotiate interest rates and closing costs just as they would with any other mortgage.

Hopefully advisers are learning how to recommend dependable lending partners, but it may take some work to find a competent lender. Unlike traditional mortgages, there are not banks and lenders for the HECM at every corner. The homeowner who lives outside metropolitan areas may have difficulty finding a lender with whom to meet face to face.

Television ads, often featuring actors and ex-Senators, do provide options. The lenders who advertise in this manner are prompt in returning your calls and emails and will send out well-crafted DVDs and colorful, easy-to-understand materials.

Just like any mortgage, advisers will be in the driver's seat if they engage with two or three lenders. Some lenders will have more discretion on loan pricing than others. In general, if the lender is a Ginnie Mae[1] issuer, the company will stand to make money on future draws from the credit line known as tails. These lenders, therefore, may be more willing to cut fees upfront, because they are banking on participating in revenue during the full length of the loan. It certainly will not hurt to ask potential lending prospects if they securitize their loans through Ginnie Mae.

Mortgage brokers can discount heavily if pushed, particularly if they are caught up in a price war with another lender. Loan originators in broker shops, however, often are paid on the opening loan balance, which could color their advice. Again, the borrower is best served in a reverse mortgage transaction by gathering bids from multiple sources.

All lenders can provide loan summary comparisons and amortization schedules demonstrating the interplay between upfront costs and home equity retention across varying interest rates. Keep in mind that the lender makes more money the higher the opening loan balance is. The profit from the secondary market on this initial "unpaid principal balance" can be quite high. This creates an incentive for lenders to originate loans with high initial draws, rather than starting with a larger line of credit.

Lenders who push for a high disbursement at closing may be thinking about their commission rather than your best interest. Even worse, some lenders suggest that the client take a large disbursement at closing, and then pay down the loan in the future. Again, this suggestion is a red flag that lenders are trying to maximize their own revenue.

Although the HECM formula for credit limits are set by the FHA via the Principal Limit factors, the amount of money that the client starts with is affected by interest rate margins and fees. The good news is that you can negotiate these elements. When applying for a traditional mortgage, clients fare better if lenders are competing for their business. The same thing is true with reverse mortgages. What homeowners negotiate will depend on how they are planning to use the HECM.

If the HECM will be in place for a short period of time

This client would want to choose a HECM with the lowest possible closing costs and no origination fee. Closing costs can be bought down by taking a higher interest rate. Just like traditional mortgages, over-par, premium pricing can be used to fund lender credits to reduce closing costs. The client can calculate how long it will take the loan balance growing at a higher rate to catch up to the reduction in upfront fees.

A client may choose this strategy in order to start an encore profession. The HECM can be paid down, or retired completely, without penalty when the business starts making money. Should he or she elect to keep the HECM in place, the LOC (just a $100 loan balance needed) would grow at an accelerated rate due to the higher interest rate.

If the HECM will be used to establish a standby line of credit

This client may benefit from taking a higher interest rate margin to buy down closing costs and lender fees. Since he or she is planning on setting up the LOC as a standby fund, this loan balance will be low and will accrue slowly. The higher interest rate margin, however, will generate higher growth in the LOC.

If the HECM is used to purchase a new principal residence

Most clients who choose to purchase a new home using the HECM select the highest possible initial credit limit. Since what they provide as their down payment is the difference between the home value and the lump sum HECM payout, they are often overly focused on the down payment, rather than the overall cost of the loan. These borrowers can benefit from negotiating with different lenders to strike the right balance between upfront fees, interest rates, and lump sum disbursements, and their own resulting down payment. Because their initial loan balance will be high and quite profitable to the lender, they are in a powerful negotiating position. Upfront mortgage insurance has been reduced on this product from 2.5% to 2.0%.

If the HECM will be used to refinance an existing traditional mortgage/HELOC

The lump sum disbursals on these loans are usually high. The client's negotiating leverage is powerful because the lender profit is substantial at the loan's outset. Again, don't be afraid to engage two or more lenders to bid for the business. If asked, the lenders will provide loan summaries and amortization schedules demonstrating the interplay between upfront costs and home equity retention based on various interest rates.

If the HECM will be disbursed in a term or tenure payment schedule

The homeowner taking a term or tenure payment will not have quite the same leverage as a full-draw, lump-sum client. Yet it is still possible to negotiate terms. Competing lenders will provide loan summaries and amortization schedules for comparison, if requested.

Negotiating interest rates and fees

The client will need to choose between taking a fixed-rate reverse mortgage or an adjustable rate. The drawback to fixed-rate loans is that they do not provide for a line of credit. Even if the loan is paid down substantially, it is considered a close-ended loan and no future draws may be taken. The Mortgage Professor expands on the differences between taking a fixed-rate traditional mortgage and a fixed-rate reverse mortgage:

> The reasons for selecting an adjustable rather than a fixed rate are also different. On a standard mortgage, few borrowers opt for an adjustable-rate because of fears that they will still have their mortgage when the initial rate period ends, and that a rate increase at that time will increase their required payment.
>
> The rationale for preferring fixed rates on standard mortgages, which is to avoid the risk of a payment increase, has no applicability to reverse mortgages, which have no required payment. The benefit of the fixed rate on a reverse mortgage is only that the borrower knows in advance exactly how fast the debt secured by his home will grow. The downside is that the fixed-rate HECM offers only one way to draw funds, which is to take a lump sum at closing. The fixed-rate HECM reverse mortgage is primarily for seniors who plan to use all or most of their borrowing power right away. Their intent is to pay off an existing mortgage, buy a house, purchase a single-premium annuity, or transact for some other purpose that requires a large and immediate payment. The fixed-rate HECM does not allow the borrower to reserve any borrowing

power for future use. Once it is closed, no more funds can be drawn.[2]

In contrast to the fixed-rate, full-draw option, the adjustable-rate HECM performs like a revolving line of credit. Payments may have been made against the loan balance. That payment is immediately available in the line of credit.

There are *three* different interest rates used in the adjustable-rate HECM:

• Note Rate

• Effective Rate

• Expected Rate

Note Rate: Adjustable-rate HECMs are configured with monthly adjusting or annually adjusting interest rates. The beginning interest rate is known as the "initial rate." This rate will adjust monthly or yearly. The new note rate will determine how much interest is accruing on the money borrowed. The monthly adjustable rate has an interest rate cap of 10%. The yearly adjustable cap is 5%.

The adjustable HECM is based today either on the one-month London Interbank Offered Rate (Libor) or the one-year Libor. This rate is known as the index. The lender adds a margin of roughly 1.5 to 4.00%. This margin can be negotiated during the application period. Higher margins are known as premium pricing and can be used to fund lender credits against closing costs. But a higher margin will generally reduce the initial credit available, so it is important to weigh the benefits of a having a larger credit limit against the growth in the line of credit. Lenders can provide amortization schedules to help make this decision.

The adjustable index rate will fluctuate with the market over the course of the loan. Once the loan is in place the margin cannot be altered by either the lender or borrower. Both the index source (Libor) and margin are locked in and can only be changed through a refinance transaction.

Table 15.1: *Effective rate (compounding rate) index + margin + MIP*

Note Rate	One-Month Libor	Varies Monthly	Lender's Margin
	One-Year Libor	Varies Yearly	1.5–4.0%
Mortgage Insurance Premium (MIP)	Set by FHA	Fixed for All HECMs	0.5%

Effective Rate: The actual rate at which the loan balance is accruing interest and MIP charges. The cost of the loan is increased by mortgage insurance premiums assessed by the FHA. In effect, adding the MIP creates an effective interest rate higher than the interest rate alone. Today the ongoing MIP rate is 0.5% annually. For example, if a client has chosen a margin of 1.8 and the one-month Libor is at 2.0% in any given month, the note rate that month is one-twelfth of 3.8 = 0.3166 per month. The actual effective rate (at which the loan balance compounds) tacks on one-twelfth of the annual MIP of 0.5% annually. Therefore, the loan balance that month will incur an effective interest rate of 2.0 + 1.8 + 0.5 = 4.3/12 = 0.358.

Expected (average) Rate: It is important to understand the implications of choosing a particular margin. The margin will affect the accumulation of interest on money borrowed, which will be the rate at which equity will be used. In addition, the margin selected for accumulating interest will be the same for the credit determinant rate (expected rate) as it is for the accrual rate (initial rate) on the loan balance. The rate used to determine initial available credit is termed the expected average rate. This rate is meant to be a predictor of the rates that will be charged over the life of the loan. Whereas the accrual rate index on monthly adjusting loans is the one-month or one-year Libor, the expected rate uses the ten-year Libor swap rate as its index. The ten-year Libor swap rate is available from the Federal Reserve.[3] *Choosing a higher margin can reduce the initial available credit.* There is, in addition, a floor below which additional credit will not be possible.

Once the loan is in place, the loan balance will compound at the effective interest rate. As shown above, the effective interest rate is the sum of the monthly applicable interest rate (note rate) plus the one-twelfth annual MIP of 0.50%.

Clients may choose a higher interest rate margin to buy down upfront fees. This could be desirable if the client intends to maintain a low loan balance and is primarily interested in maximizing growth in the HECM line of credit.

FHA counseling is mandatory before application: How to find a counselor

There is an important consumer safeguard to protect borrowers from mistakenly concluding that, because there are no payments, the reverse mortgage is something other than debt. Potential borrowers must complete a counseling session before making an application with a lender. Counselors review the loan obligations and emphasize that taxes and insurance are the responsibility of the borrower. Likewise, the counselors explain that the loan is accumulating interest and FHA mortgage insurance premiums, which will need to be paid back when the last participant dies, moves, or sells.[4]

Finding a lender

The National Reverse Mortgage Lenders Association maintains a lender search tool. Use the search tool to locate lenders by state (specifically the state in which the property is located). All lenders are members of the National Reverse Mortgage Lenders Association, are licensed to originate reverse mortgages in the states in which they are listed, and have signed NRMLA's Code of Conduct & Professional Responsibility.[5]

Filing a complaint

Complaints may be submitted to the Consumer Financial Protection Bureau at www.consumerfinance.gov/complaint.

Phone: (855) 411-CFPB (2372)

TTY/TDD: (855) 729-CFPB (2372)

For those who already have a reverse mortgage

Regulations have changed on how someone living in the house, but not on the loan documents, will be treated once the primary borrower leaves the house permanently. The CFPB recommends doing the following three things if you or your loved ones have a reverse mortgage:

1. Verify who is on the loan. If you took out a reverse mortgage with two borrowers, check with your reverse mortgage to make sure its loan records are accurate. Call your servicer to find out what names are listed on your loan. They may be able to help you over the phone. See your reverse mortgage statement for the phone number, and ask them to send you this information in writing for your records. You can also write a letter requesting information.

2. If your reverse mortgage is in the name of only one spouse, make a plan for the non-borrowing spouse. Contact your loan servicer to find out if the non-borrowing spouse can qualify for a repayment deferral. A repayment deferral allows a non-borrowing spouse to remain living in the home after the death of the borrowing spouse. If not, make a plan in the event

the borrowing spouse dies first and the loan becomes due. If you or your spouse are not on the loan but believe that you should be, promptly seek legal advice. If you have enough remaining equity in your home, you could consider taking out a new reverse mortgage with both spouses. You'll have to pay loan fees again, however, for the new loan. If the non-borrowing spouse can't pay off the reverse mortgage when the borrowing spouse passes away, he or she might consider a new traditional mortgage if they have the income and credit to qualify. Also consider other family members who would be willing to cosign on such a loan. Some surviving spouses may need to sell the home and make plans for where they will live after the home is sold. Contact a HUD-approved counselor to discuss options.

3. Talk to your children and heirs—make a plan for any non-borrowing members living in the house.[6]

Other red flags

The CFPB reports that mortgages of all kinds generate the highest number of complaints to that agency. Complaints on reverse mortgages are relatively rare. From December 1, 2011, through December 31, 2014, CFPB handled approximately 1,200 reverse mortgage complaints. Reverse mortgage complaints comprise about 1% of all mortgage complaints, regardless of age, submitted to the CFPB. Consumers' most frequent complaints involve their inability to make certain changes to the loans, as well as loan servicing difficulties.[7] Although servicers do provide monthly statements, they are opaque in the extreme. And unfortunately, those answering the phone are often poorly trained and cannot explain most of what is printed on the statement.

As in the traditional mortgage world, certain behaviors could indicate that your best interests are not being considered. Any lender that pushes you to make a rash decision cannot be trusted. If requested by the homeowner, ethical lenders are only too happy to meet with the adult children, financial adviser, CPA, banker, or others to help improve comprehension of how the HECM works. Lenders that encourage taking out larger lump sums than needed likely are focusing on their commissions. Lenders that decline to provide a variety of loan summary comparisons and accompanying amortization schedules for both adjustable-rate and fixed-rate options with a full range of interest rate choices are not serving your best interest. Lenders that push for fixed-rate, full-draw loans may be motivated by the profit on the sale of the note on the secondary market.

Some lenders are agnostic in the way they compensate their loan officers. This means that regardless of how the money is disbursed, the loan officer is paid at a set rate. Other lenders incent their loan officers based on the initial draw taken at closing. You certainly are entitled to ask how commissions are computed.

If a loan officer states that the HECM line of credit is earning interest, he or she is either being deceptive or does not understand that the amount available to be borrowed from the HECM line of credit increases over time. The HECM LOC increase is just an opportunity to borrow more against home equity. The amount of increase is dependent upon the interest rate, as described earlier, but no interest is earned by the borrower on an LOC.

On rare occasions, some financial planners have colluded with lenders to use a client's home equity inappropriately. Be wary of any third party who is linking any mortgage, reverse mortgages included, to other financial products. Housing wealth may not be used to buy securities. Securities can lose value and the client would have lost home equity by embarking on a mortgage, a reverse mortgage included. This situation would be a double whammy and is not permissible.

Conclusion

An adviser can provide critical advice in differentiating offerings from reverse mortgage companies as long as they are not prohibited by their employer from doing so. Never take the first offer. Compare lenders and take your time deciding!

Notes

1   The Government National Mortgage Association (GNMA), or Ginnie Mae. A government corporation within the Department of Housing and Urban Development (HUD), Ginnie Mae's mission is to expand affordable housing.

The Ginnie Mae guarantee allows mortgage lenders to obtain a better price for their loans in the capital markets. Lenders then can use the proceeds to make new mortgage loans available to consumers.

2   http://www.mtgprofessor.com/A%20-%20Reverse%20 Mortgages/adjustable_rate_versus_fixed_rate.html.

3   http://www.federalreserve.gov/releases/h15/update/.

4   HUD-approved counselors can be found at http://www.hud.gov/offices/hsg/sfh/hcc/hcs.cfm.

5   http://www.reversemortgage.org/FindaLender.aspx.

6   https://www.consumerfinance.gov/blog/consumer-advisory-three-steps-you-should-take-if-you-have-a-reverse-mortgage/.

7   https://files.consumerfinance.gov/f/201502_cfpb_report_ snapshot-reverse-mortgage-complaints-december-2011-2014.pdf.

SIXTEEN

The Application Process

Once the client has obtained a counseling certificate and chosen a lender, an application is taken by a loan officer, either in person or on the phone. Commonly, the applicant provides an appraisal fee (less than $500) at application. The interest rate that applies to determining credit (expected rate) will be frozen for a short period of time. At closing, whichever rate provides the highest Principal Limit, either the current expected rate or the expected rate at application, will be used. The initial accrual interest rate will be tied to that week's one-month or one-year Libor, if it is a monthly adjustable-rate HECM. In an effort to reduce appraisal bias, which ultimately can compromise the FHA insurance fund recovery of equity, the FHA may request a second appraisal.

The appraisal

An FHA-approved appraiser will schedule a visit to assess the home, both inside and out. Over the next few weeks, the homeowner will be asked to provide documents illustrating his or her financial situation. Gathering as many of these documents as possible before application can reduce stress during the process. Anyone who has taken out a traditional home loan knows how irritating the escalating requests for documents can be, not to mention being asked two or three times for the same information. Needless to say, the client should keep a copy of every document sent to the mortgage company.

Should the appraisal come back lower than expected, the homeowner can appeal. Sometimes properties themselves are ineligible for FHA lending. Competent loan officers are adept at avoiding these mistakes. It is against the law, however, for a lender to refuse to take an application for credit if the borrower so wishes. Today, FHA may require a second appraisal in an effort to monitor appraisal irregularities.

Underwriting and the life-expectancy set-aside (LESA)

Since April 2015, applicants are required to undergo a financial assessment. The financial assessment will determine whether or not a potential borrower meets willingness and capacity qualifiers. If the applicant's past credit history does not demonstrate willingness to meet homeowner obligations, HECM regulations require that that a portion of his or her proceeds be placed in a fully funded life-expectancy set-aside (LESA). This set-aside is based on life expectancy and the total predicted tax and insurance payments for the future. It is possible that the LESA could be so high the borrower will not qualify for the HECM. For others, this set-aside is a relief. They are happy to have someone else make sure that their taxes and insurance payments are made.

If the applicant can demonstrate willingness, but does not meet residual income guidelines, HECM guidelines require a partially funded set-aside. The partial funding is for applicants who meet the credit requirements of willingness but may struggle to have enough cash flow to make tax and insurance payments. This set-aside, which can be much smaller, is used to draw funds from the HECM twice a year. The lender sends the funds to the borrower who is responsible for satisfying the tax and insurance obligations.

Processing

Once the application is approved, a lawyer's office or title company will complete a title search and issue title insurance. Homeowner's insurance is required. Flood insurance may be as well. All of these closing costs, including various state and local taxes, will be assessed along with upcoming property taxes. These borrower costs will be deducted from available funds, technically known as the "Net Principal Limit" unless they are paid upfront. These fees, if not paid up front, become part of the beginning loan balance.

Closing

Just as you would for any mortgage closing, you should insist on studying the HUD-1 closing document before attending the closing. The last thing you want to do is see the numbers for the first time under the pressure of sitting in an unfamiliar office with countless papers to sign. Fortunately, loans that are considered a refinance (not purchase loans) require a three-day right of rescission. If you have requested a disbursal at closing, those funds will be made available at the end of the rescission period. In a few weeks, the loan servicer will be in touch with you to arrange for scheduled payments and/or line of credit draws.

Servicing

The lender may or may not service the loan. This is a standard practice in mortgage lending,[1] and clients can expect servicing to change hands. It is important to watch for notices advising that this relationship has changed. Notices are required by law to precede a change.

The servicer will send the homeowner monthly statements indicating loan balance, interest rate changes, draws, available line of credit, and voluntary payments received. The statements will include servicer contact information.

Note

1   For a discussion of the difference between a servicer and a lender, see https://www.consumerfinance.gov/ask-cfpb/ whats-the-difference-between-a-mortgage-lender-and-a-servicer-en-198/.

SEVENTEEN

Nuts And Bolts: Typical FAQs

The best way to start understanding reverse mortgages is to engage with lenders. They will email/mail easy-to-digest information on how reverse mortgages work. Ask for an individual proposal based on your age and home value covering a variety of interest rate margins and draw patterns. If your home is expensive or not FHA-insurable, you will want to research online for companies that offer proprietary reverse mortgages in your state, sometimes known as Jumbos.

The mortgage company will provide the potential borrower with a copy of *Use Your Home to Stay at Home* published by the National Council on Aging.[1] What follows is a typical summation of homeowner qualifications, property eligibility, and other basic components of FHA HECM lending provided by lenders and NRMLA:

Who qualifies and what properties are eligible?

One homeowner must be at least sixty-two years of age. Eligible properties include single-family homes, FHA-approved condominiums, and multi-family structures with up to four units.

What if one person is sixty-two and the other is sixty-eight?

The age of the youngest person is used.

Does my credit matter and is a credit report required?

Yes, a credit report is required. The lender is looking for federal liens and evidence that property obligations have been met in the past. Any federal lien would need to be satisfied before the HECM could be used. Credit scores don't matter but payment history is analyzed.

What if I have a bankruptcy or tax lien on my credit report?

Unlike a traditional mortgage, a HECM is not provided based on credit scores alone. A Chapter 7 Bankruptcy appearing on your credit report will need to have been discharged prior to closing. A Chapter 13 Bankruptcy appearing on your credit report must show a satisfactory payment history and may possibly have to be paid through closing. You may also need to provide a letter of explanation for these matters.

Is the rate fixed or variable?

You can choose fixed or variable. However, a fixed rate can be chosen only where the entire amount of initial available credit is drawn at the outset. This results in a high balance and does not allow for a revolving credit line.

What is the HECM counseling certificate?

FHA requires each applicant to complete a counseling session with an independent third-party counselor over the phone. The counselor will ask you questions and answer any questions you have to confirm your understanding of the HECM program. After this session a counseling certificate will be issued showing completion.

What are the closing costs?

The closing costs are similar to those of a regular FHA mortgage. A mortgage insurance premium (MIP) is established and is based on the appraised value of the home. There are also third-party fees like title, appraisal, and recording.

Who owns title to the home?

The borrower is fully vested on the title of the home. You can never lose title to your home so long as taxes, insurance, and any homeowner association dues are kept current. Additionally, the home must remain in good condition and serve as your primary residence.

What if I decide to sell my house in ten years and the house has depreciated and I owe more than what I can sell it for?

It's not your problem. The house will be sold for fair market value and the proceeds will pay off the mortgage. Any deficit will be paid by FHA to the lender.

Isn't the HECM just another program that will end up getting the federal government in trouble?

No, this is not a taxpayer-funded program. Every person who acquires an FHA-insured loan contributes to the FHA mortgage insurance fund. In the case of regular (non-HECM) FHA mortgage insured loans, part of the borrower's monthly payment goes toward the FHA mortgage insurance fund. In the case of the HECM program, the lender pays FHA 0.50% of the loan balance per year (which in turn accrues on the loan balance), which creates a continuous stream of dollars to the insurance fund.

What happens when both spouses die?

The house will be left to the estate and will be settled the exact same way as any other estate with a house involved. An appraised value will be determined and the house will be sold for fair market value. If the sale price exceeds the mortgage balance, the difference will go to the estate. If the sale price is less than the mortgage balance, the estate will *not* be responsible for that deficit.

Isn't this program only for people who don't have money?

The program is used by middle-income earners as well as millionaires. It allows financially savvy people to use the value of their home as an additional source of retirement assets instead of leaving it tied up, illiquid and unavailable, while still fully retaining the shelter and enjoyment of the home.

How does the bank/lender make its money?

On a traditional mortgage the bank receives interest as part of the monthly payment. The HECM interest accrues in the background, causing the balance to grow over time. The bank or investor makes money on the total interest accrued at the time the house is sold.

What property types are excluded?

Co-ops are currently excluded. A HECM may not attach to a vacation home or investment property. Condos are permitted if an FHA condo approval can be obtained. Multi-family homes may be eligible if the borrower lives there.

Is there a limit on the amount of funds you can access during the initial year?

If you are eligible for a $100,000 loan, for example, you can take $60,000, or 60% of that sum. There are exceptions. You can withdraw a bit more if you have an existing mortgage, or other liens on the property, that exceed the 60% limit. You must pay off these "mandatory obligations" as the FHA terms them, and this is usually done with the proceeds from the HECM. You can withdraw enough to pay off these obligations, plus another 10% of the maximum allowable amount—in which case that's an extra $10,000, or 10% of $100,000. You are permitted to exceed the 60% limit if you are using the HECM to purchase a new principal residence. Loan proceeds can be taken as a lump sum, as a line of credit, or as fixed monthly payments, either for a fixed amount of time or for as long as you remain in the home. You can also combine these options; for example, taking part of the proceeds as a lump sum and leaving the balance in a line of credit. Fees can be paid out of the loan proceeds. This means you incur very little out-of-pocket expense to get a reverse mortgage. Your only out-of-pocket expense is the appraisal fee and possibly a charge for counseling, depending on the counseling organization you work with. Together, these two fees will total a few hundred dollars. Very low-income homeowners are exempted from counseling charges. When you ultimately pay off the loan, the final balance equals the amount of funds borrowed, plus annual mortgage insurance premiums, servicing fees and interest. The loan balance grows while you are living in the home. In other words, when you sell or leave the house, you owe more than you originally borrowed.

Look at it this way: A traditional mortgage is a balloon full of air that gets smaller each time you make a payment. A reverse mortgage is an empty balloon that grows larger as time passes. With a HECM, no matter how large the loan balance, you never have to pay more than the appraised value of the home or the sale price. This feature is referred to as "non-recourse." If the loan balance exceeds the appraised value of the home, then the FHA insurance fund absorbs that loss. You are responsible for paying property taxes, homeowner insurance, condo fees, and other financial charges. Any lapse in these policies can trigger a default on your loan. To help reduce future defaults, the FHA requires lenders to conduct a financial assessment of all prospective borrowers. Lenders will analyze all income sources—including pensions, Social Security, IRAs, and 401(k) plans—as well as your credit history. They will look closely at how much money is left over after paying typical living expenses. If a lender determines that you have sufficient income left over, then you won't have to worry about having funds set aside for future tax and insurance payments. If, however, a lender determines that you may not be able to keep up with property taxes and insurance payments, they will be authorized to set aside a certain amount of funds from your loan to pay future charges.[2]

Notes

1   For a downloadable copy: https://www.ncoa.org/economic-security/home-equity/housing-options/use-your-home-to-stay-at-home.

2   http://www.reversemortgage.org/About/FeaturesofReverseMortgages.aspx.

EIGHTEEN

Robert C. Merton, Nobel Laureate: Reverse Mortgages Around The World

It was quite exciting to us in the reverse mortgage business when we learned that Dr. Robert C. Merton was traveling the world extolling the concept of reverse mortgages. Dr. Merton is the School of Management Distinguished Professor of Finance at MIT Sloan and University Professor Emeritus at Harvard University. Dr. Merton received the Alfred Nobel Memorial Prize in Economic Sciences in 1997 for developing a new method to determine the value of derivatives. He is past president of the American Finance Association, a member of the National Academy of Sciences, and a Fellow of the American Academy of Arts and Sciences. I have had the honor of meeting Dr. Merton twice and I can tell you that his interest in reverse mortgages springs from a genuine desire to help aging people around the world have what he calls a *good retirement*. Admittedly he is looking for an innovative way to finance reverse mortgages but this does not lessen his commitment to the mission to help retirees liberate their home equity while still enjoying the comfort and safety of their homes. Home ownership rates for retirees in many countries are even higher than in the US (80%+). Longevity in other countries can be significantly longer in other countries, as well, which just underscores how crucial equity release in retirement is globally. One thing that you notice when reading about financial products outside the US is the use of the word "scheme." This word does not have the same negative connotation as it does to Americans!

In honor of Dr. Merton, here is a quick review of reverse mortgages across the world. Thank you to Masahiro Kobayashi, Shoichiro Konishi, and Toshihiko Takeishi for access to their informative paper, "The Reverse Mortgage Market in Japan and its Challenges," from which some of the content below was taken.[1]

UK

I begin with the UK because I visited the Equity Release Council in London in 2016. Apparently, the equity release concept is gaining in popularity. Over 37,000 new customers entered an equity release plan in 2017, with almost 67,000 new and existing customers making withdrawals of housing wealth in total that year (Equity Release Council, January 2018). Homeowners are eligible at age fifty-five, versus sixty-two here in the US. There are two types of reverse mortgages, the Lifetime Mortgage and the Home Reversion Plan. The Lifetime Mortgage walls off (ring-fences) a portion of equity, if the homeowner chooses, that cannot be invaded with rolling up interest charges. The homeowner is protected by the No Negative Equity Guarantee (NNEG). More equity could be released for those with certain medical conditions. Payments on the Lifetime Mortgage are voluntary. With the Home Reversion Plan, homeowners relinquish all or some of the home's equity in return for a lump sum or payments with the absolute guarantee that they can live there rent-free without interference until they die. At the end, the house is sold, and the proceeds are divided according to percentage of ownership. Again, health can influence the terms, a concept not embraced in the US system.

The Equity Release Council holds financial adviser providers to strict standards of conduct including acting "with the best interests of their clients being paramount, treating customers fairly in all their actions." This is quite a different approach than in the US where reverse mortgages are provided by mortgage brokers, lenders, and banks. Financial advisers in the US are pretty much frozen out of the transaction and are even prevented by their compliance departments from discussing equity release.[2]

Canada

The reverse mortgage program in Canada is known as CHIP (Canadian Home Income Plan) and is advertised heavily, and with some humor, by HomeEquity Bank. In British Columbia, Alberta, and Ontario urban areas, the PATH Home Plan is offered by Equitable Bank. The first thing to notice is that potential borrowers are warned to be careful that they are reading about the Canadian reverse mortgage and *not* the US one. Although the two programs have the same safeguards, the US internet and press love to beat up on the US version. Apparently Canadians do not share the same vitriol for equity release products. One site states that you "remain on title to the home, and you can never owe more than the value of the home. As long as you are still living there, you can never be forced to move or sell. These protections are guaranteed in writing." These are the same exact safeguards provided with the FHA-insured HECM, so we again are left wondering why the negative reputation persists for the HECM in the US. The Canadian version can begin at age fifty-five. The Canadian reverse mortgage is growing in uptake, again another difference. One website says "Save on taxes! You can use a Canadian Reverse Mortgage to take cash out of the home and put it into investments. All the interest charged on the loan is then tax deductible." This is certainly a different take as using reverse mortgage proceeds for investment in the US is forbidden.

South Korea

Next we move on to our friends in South Korea, who have the best name for a reverse mortgage: Home Pension. The reverse mortgage there enjoys all the same protections provided by the HECM and is guaranteed by the Korea

Housing Finance Corporation. KHFC-sponsored reverse mortgages provide an incentive to reduce property taxes by 25%. The Korean system allows access at age sixty, even though the Korean lifespan is longer than the US lifespan. The interest rates are lower than on traditional mortgages.

Japan

In 2005, the Tokyo Star Bank introduced a "collateralized deposits reverse mortgage" and charged 0% interest until withdrawals equaled deposits. This was a popular offering and other banks followed. The Japanese Housing Finance Agency offers an "Exceptional Repayment Schedule for Elderlies" that can be used to improve home safety and accessibility. Monthly interest payments are required and then repaid at death with proceeds from the sale of the home. The interest rates are quite low. A critical difference from the HECM is an allowance of a one-time payment for the senior to live in rental housing that provides nursing services. Not all programs offered in Japan are non-recourse and some require the heirs to repay the reverse mortgage proceeds that are not recovered by the sale of the house. Some lenders require heirs to provide consent for the reverse mortgage in order to avoid inheritance issues.

Australia

Australia is struggling with an aging population as well as a tight housing market and the reverse mortgage market is growing rapidly. The Australian government offered older Australians lucrative incentives to downsize and free up housing stock, but the measure was not popular. Reverse mortgages in Australia are not government-insured as is the HECM. However, the government does offer an income stream reverse mortgage, and in 2018 the federal government announced they would broaden this scheme. The interest rate on the federal scheme is 5.25%, approximately 1% lower than rates from commercial providers, who have broader criteria and products with more flexibility. Reverse mortgages are heavily regulated in Australia. Commercial providers include Heartland Seniors Finance (a NRMLA member who is also the leading provider in New Zealand). Its website touts an NNEG as well as an equity protection option that allows a quarantine of a percentage of the eventual sale of the home.[3] Interestingly, there is a provision for use of a secondary property for security. The percentage of home value that may be borrowed is drastically lower than the HECM but home prices in Australia are very high. Household Capital suggests integrating longevity income from the home with superannuation and the government pension.

New Zealand

The reverse mortgages offered are private, not government-insured as is the HECM. The amount of equity that is accessible is 15%–50%. Benefits can begin at age sixty. Payment options include a lump sum or regular income. Some equity may be set aside. Unlike the HECM, there is not specific legal protection for borrowers other than general protection under the Consumer Guarantees Act. Most lenders comply with the Responsible Lending Code although it is not binding. The Ministry of Social Development and Commission for Financial Capability recommend that the borrower seek independent legal and financial advice. This is different than the US which requires homeowners to obtain a counseling certificate from an independent FHA-approved agency.

China

In 2014 the government launched a government-backed reverse mortgage named the "House for Pension." This program allows the homeowner to mortgage property to an insurance company. Apparently, the uptake has been quite slow—not surprising since a survey by the Central China Normal University indicated that 98% of the children of seniors were against their parents taking a monthly pension in the form of a reverse mortgage. The reverse mortgage has at least one fan, though—Meng Xiaosu, known as the godfather of real estate. The graying population will face the problems lingering from the one-child policy and will stress government social programs. Mr. Meng is concerned that the elderly will suffer. He helped create the House for Pension program offered by Happy Life Insurance, one of two insurers in the market, but fewer than one hundred people have participated.

Singapore

Home ownership rates in Singapore are extremely high, over 90%. Most of the homes are public housing for which homeowners are granted a ninety-nine-year lease. The house reverts back to the government at the end of the lease. The Housing and Development Board is exploring a Lease Buyback Scheme (LBS) to help retirees monetize their property. It is designed to work in conjunction with the pension fund, the Central Provident Fund. Money freed up from housing through the LBS is credited to the homeowner's CPF account. Elderly CPF members receive lifelong monthly payouts based on their choice of annuity purchased using their CPF retirement balances. Interestingly, Singapore is leading the world in finding ways to help the elderly stay connected with other generations. The *Wall Street Journal* reports that:

> The city-state has launched a multibillion-dollar effort to create a *"kampong* for all ages," embracing the Malay word for village in an effort to build "a cohesive society with intergenerational harmony." … Officials are launching initiatives to have preschools share facilities with senior centers, recruit young people to teach technology to older people, and help organizations better use older volunteers. Since 2013 they've been building and promoting "3Gen flats," designed for families to house grandparents and grandchildren under one roof. They're also spending about $150 million to underwrite an innovation challenge to seek new ideas and research that promote productive aging.[4]

Italy

There are a sprinkling of reverse mortgage structures in Italy. One requires the homeowner to live in a municipality of more than 30,000 people. Some providers require that the homeowner pay interest and expenses monthly.

France

The viager contract has existed for decades and is a contract between two private parties. This is what Madame Calment arranged with the lawyer next door. It usually involves a lump sum "bouquet" and a monthly payment for life. The seller remains in the property. Should the buyer default, the seller keeps the bouquet and all the monthly payments and recovers title to the property. There are products called reverse mortgages in France but they require payments and have restrictions on what the money is used for, so they do not conform to our idea of a reverse mortgage. It is possible to take an interest-only loan, but again there are qualifying uses. The loan must be repaid by the time the borrower is seventy-five to eighty years old.

Spain

Spain is struggling with its pension system and is considering extending the retirement age. The reverse mortgage in Spain is known as a "lifetime loan." Homeowners are eligible at age sixty-five or if they have a serious disability. One site notes that expats can manage currency inequities by placing a reverse mortgage on their property which will pay in Euros. The Óptima Mayores website describes equity released in the form of monthly payments.[5] An insurer will take over the monthly payments should the homeowner survive a "certain age." The borrower can never owe more than the home's value.

Conclusion

If you are like me, you found it interesting to see how other countries approach home equity wealth for their huge aging populations. Like me, you may have concluded that in comparison our HECM is amazingly generous, readily available to all, free of restrictions, and extraordinarily flexible.

Notes

1   M Kobayashi, S Konishi and T Takeishi,
    "The Reverse Mortgage Market in Japan and its Challenges",
    Cityscope, www.huduser.gov/portal/periodicals/cityscpe/
    vol19num1/article5.html.

2   www.equityreleasecouncil.com/standards/statement-of-
    principles.

3   www.seniorsfinance.com.au.

4   www.wsj.com/articles/building-bridges-across-the-
    generational-divide-1541086302.

5   http://floorclausereclaim.com/index.php/news/blog/116-
    blog-011-lifetime-loans-or-reverse-mortgages-in-spain.

NINETEEN

Conclusion:
Do Not Wait

The HECM reverse mortgage has evolved to meet the needs of mainstream America. The original intent of the program was to help retirees liquidate home wealth throughout retirement, as needed. But when equity consumption ran off the rails in the housing bubble, the program, and individuals ill-suited for reverse mortgages, suffered. In response, the FHA has restructured the program to encourage using it in a conservative and prudent fashion.

Whether or not an individual homeowner elects to consume housing wealth is a decision best made with facts and thoughtful analysis, not emotions and half-baked preconceptions. It could be a costly mistake to ignore the protections a reverse mortgage can provide, particularly over a thirty- to forty-year retirement.

Peter Neuwirth, FSA, FCA often reminds me how present value considerations assist us in making decisions today while keeping in mind what may happen in the future.

Steve Vernon, FSA, another actuary and Research Scholar at the Stanford Center for Longevity, warns that to make effective decisions for retirement requires imagining one's future self—not an easy thing to do. Many people just avoid making financial decisions altogether. If you choose not think about it, the cost to you in the future of not having established at least an LOC on your house could be high. The randomness of what the future holds may help you decide whether or not your personal approach to retirement planning will include using your home.

There are some very good reasons to not wait until you *need* one to apply for a reverse mortgage:

- If you wait for portfolio ruin, your financial situation may have deteriorated to such a degree that, under new financial assessment rules, you will not be able to qualify.[1]

- If you do not set up a HECM LOC early in retirement, you lose the compounding growth of a liquid asset.

- If you do not set up a HECM LOC early in retirement, it cannot serve as an alternate source of income should you encounter a dangerous early sequence of bad investment returns.

- Because interest rates are low today, the initial credit limit is high. If you wait until you need a reverse mortgage, rates may be significantly higher, and consequently your credit limit could be substantially lower. This could prevent you from replacing a traditional mortgage (with monthly payments) with a HECM just when you need it most.

- Because your house is an undiversified asset, placing a guaranteed, growing LOC on it allows you to hedge against declining housing values.

The ultimate interest-only mortgage

So, for the reader, I offer what I would do early in retirement with my own home. I would open a HECM line of credit with a minimum balance. I would accomplish this by choosing a higher interest rate margin. By taking a higher rate, I would be able to negotiate with my lender to avoid incurring an origination fee. The ongoing interest and MIP costs for this minimum balance would be modest; I would just let the LOC grow and not use the available funds unless a clear need arose. Thus, my reverse mortgage is functioning as a *standby emergency fund, the giant shock absorber.*

Now here is what is important to me as I imagine my future self. If I did need to draw substantial funds from the HECM, say to avoid drawing on my portfolio at a loss, I would treat the HECM as if it were an interest-only loan. This means that I would make voluntary payments on the accruing interest and MIP to keep the loan balance low, and the compounding interest under control. In other words, I would have the use of the amount borrowed, tax-free, but would avoid the compounding that can accumulate so quickly with a reverse mortgage.

Only a reverse mortgage allows this flexibility. By setting up a HECM, there is no commitment to any particular loan amount nor a prescribed repayment schedule. It is my choice how to use the money, how to allow interest to accrue, or not, and how to pay the loan back.

You can see that my plan is conservative. Keeping the loan balance low would give me the most flexibility if I wanted to move later in retirement and needed equity from my home to make the move. Again, imagining my future self, if I lived very long in my house, and I could not make the interest payments comfortably, I would change my strategy and start letting the interest accrue. In other words, if bad stuff happened, I would fall back on the non-recourse guarantee that the house, not me, would pay the loan back. So I have converted the risk for falling property values and my own longevity to the FHA mortgage insurance pool, not me or my estate. I would be at peace with this outcome, because like every other HECM customer, I contributed to the mortgage insurance fund for this very protection.

After years in the industry, this is the scenario that I have decided would work for me. Everyone is different, and encumbering the home with debt is never a decision to be made rashly. Yet above all it is a decision deserving to be made with facts, not fabrications.

Perhaps you note a bit of fanaticism on my part? Without getting overwrought, I admit that I am on a mission to inform US retirees, and those they trust for financial advice, about how a reverse mortgage really works, how much it really costs, and how it can help other assets.

I thank you, the reader, for opening your mind to what must have seemed an unlikely topic. I hope that you agree now that yes, a reverse mortgage isn't for everybody, but it isn't wrong for anybody, either.[2]

Notes

1 Thank you to Mark Schumacher for this observation. Private Correspondence.

2 David W. Johnson, PhD, is an associate professor of finance at the University of Wisconsin. By permission of David Johnson.

Resources

HUD HECM Handbook (4235.1)
https://www.hud.gov/program_offices/administration/
hudclips/handbooks/hsgh/4235.1

HUD/FHA Mortgagee Letters
https://www.hudexchange.info/programs/housing-counseling/
hecm/mortgagee-letters

Active Adult Living 55+ Communities
http://activeadultliving.com

Aging in Place Ideas
www.louistenenbaum.com

Aging in Place Technology Watch
www.ageinplacetech.com

AlphaEngine Global Investment Solutions, LLC
http://www.alphaengine.net/aboutus.html

**American College of Financial Services Retirement Income
Certified Professional degree**
https://ricp.theamericancollege.edu

American Society on Aging
www.asaging.org

Anna Rappaport Consulting
http://annarappaport.com

Barbara Stucki, Consultant
www.linkedin.com/pub/barbara-stucki/6/548/471

Blue Ocean Global Wealth
www.blueoceanglobalwealth.com

Calculator for Determining HECM Funds Available
www.newretirement.com

Christopher J. Mayer, PhD, Paul Milstein Professor of Real Estate at Columbia Business School

https://www0.gsb.columbia.edu/faculty/cmayer

Consumer Financial Protection Bureau

www.consumerfinance.gov

Curtis Cloke, LUTC, LUTCF, RICP

http://curtiscloke.com/thrive-university.html

Deborah Lucas, PhD, Sloan Distinguished Professor of Finance at MIT's Sloan School of Management

http://mitsloan.mit.edu/faculty-and-research/faculty-directory/detail/?id=41235

Dinkytown.net Financial Calculators

www.dinkytown.com

Elder Index of Economic Security

www.ncoa.org/economic-security/money-management/elder-index

Eldercare Locator

www.eldercare.gov or 1-800-677-1116

Family Caregiver Alliance

www.caregiver.org

Fannie Mae Study on HECM: The Secondary Market Investor Experience

https://papers.ssrn.com/sol3/papers.cfm?abstract_id=3055881

Financial Planning Association

www.plannersearch.org

FINRA BrokerCheck

https://brokercheck.finra.org

HECM for Purchase Calculator, Ibis Software

http://rmc.ibisreverse.com/rmc_pages/rmc_hfhp/rmc_hfhp_1.aspx

HECM Retirement Calculators, Mutual of Omaha Bank Retirement Funding Solutions
www.rfslends.com/tools

Holland Financial
http://planstronger.com

Home Care Association of America
www.hcaoa.org

International Retirement Resource Center
https://www.retirement-resource-center.com

Jamie Hopkins, MBA, JD
www.hopkinsretirement.com

Laurie Goodman, PhD, Urban Institute
www.urban.org/author/laurie-goodman

Maximizing Social Security Retirement Benefits, by Mary Beth Franklin (eBook)
https://home.investmentnews.com/clickshare/selectItems.
do?CSCategory=maxSocSecBenefit&CSPTrack=booktore

Michael Falk, CFA, Focus Consulting Group Inc.
http://www.focuscgroup.com/about-us/michael-falk

Michael E. Kitces MSFS, MTAX, CFP®, CLU, ChFC, RHU, REBC, CASL
www.kitces.com

Mortgage Professor
www.mtgprofessor.com

NAIFA Limited and Extended Care Planning Center
https://naifa.lifehappenspro.org/about

National Academy of Elder Law Attorneys
www.naela.org

National Aging and Disability Transportation Center
https://www.nadtc.org

National Association of Area Agencies on Aging
www.n4a.org

National Association of Insurance and Financial Advisors
www.naifa.org/about-naifa

National Association of Personal Financial Advisors
https://napfa.org

National Council on Aging (NCOA)
www.ncoa.org

National Reverse Mortgage Lenders Association (NRMLA) Lender Directory
www.reversemortgage.org/FindaLender.aspx

NCOA Booklet *Use Your Home to Stay at Home* **(Downloadable)**
www.ncoa.org/wp-content/uploads/FINAL-2018-NCOA-Reverse-Mortgage-Booklet.pdf

NewRetirement
www.newretirement.com

NRMLA Guide for Finding a Counselor
www.reversemortgage.org/YourRoadmap/3Counseling.aspx

NRMLA HECM Calculator
www.reversemortgage.org/About/ReverseMortgageCalculator.aspx

Peter Neuwirth, FSA, FCA
www.peterneuwirth.com

Professional Mortgage Alliance
www.professionalmortgagealliance.com

Robert Merton, PhD, MIT Sloan School of Management Distinguished Professor of Finance
https://mitsloan.mit.edu/faculty/directory/robert-c-merton

Sandra Timmermann, EdD, Gerontology Consulting/Aging and Business Strategies

sandratimmermann1@gmail.com

Seniors Real Estate Specialists® of the National Association of Realtors©

www.seniorsrealestate.com

Social Security Detailed Benefit Calculator

http://socialsecurity.gov/OACT/anypia/anypia.html

Stephanie Moulton, Associate Professor, Director of Doctoral Studies, John Glenn College of Public Affairs, Ohio State University

http://glenn.osu.edu/faculty/glenn-faculty/moulton

Steve Vernon, FSA

stevevernon.com

Steven W. Thomas, CLU, ChFC, LUTCF

www.planamerica.biz/about

Texas Tech University Department of Personal Financial Planning

www.depts.ttu.edu/pfp

Thomas Davidoff, Associate Professor, Strategy and Business Economics Division, UBC Sauder School of Business

www.sauder.ubc.ca/Faculty/People/Faculty_Members/Davidoff_Thomas

Thomas C. B. Davison, MA, PhD, CFP®, Tools for Retirement Planning

http://toolsforretirementplanning.com

Wade Pfau, PhD, CFA, Professor of Retirement Income at The American College

http://retirementresearcher.com

Women's Institute For A Secure Retirement

www.wiserwomen.org

Glossary

Adjustable-Rate HECM An option selected by the home-owner. The index rate can change either monthly or annually. HECM adjustable-rate loans can be indexed to either the Treasury (CMT) rate or the London Interbank Offered Rate (Libor). A given loan must use either Treasury or Libor for both the Initial and the Expected Rates. Some lenders offer a monthly adjusting HECM with a 5% lifetime cap increase. The annually adjusting HECM uses the one-year Libor rate as its index. It generally has a 2% cap on annual changes and a 5% lifetime cap.

Amortization The process of paying off debt with payments allotted to carrying costs (interest) and principal.

Annuitize A right to receive periodic payments, usually fixed in size, for life or a term of years that is created by a contract or other legal document. The HECM Tenure Payment Option annuitizes a portion of the house.

Bankruptcy Lender shall have no obligation to make further loan advances on or following the date that a petition for bankruptcy of borrower is filed. At application Chapter 7 or Chapter 11 bankruptcies must be discharged or dismissed. If the credit report says that the bankruptcy was dismissed or discharged more than a year ago, no additional documents are required. If it was dismissed or discharged less than a year ago or if the credit report does not show a dismissal, a court order signed by a judge or a credit supplement evidencing the discharge or dismissal may be submitted as proof of the discharge or dismissal. Chapter 13 may pay the bankruptcy off at the closing or continue with the bankruptcy and the reverse mortgage. The borrower still has to pay off any liens against the property and any federal debt. The borrower will need permission from the court to do so.

Cap An upper limit on the interest rate that applies to a loan, (e.g., an adjustable-rate mortgage).

Combination Payment Option Selecting one or more payment options to be used simultaneously.

Co-ops Cooperatives were authorized by Congress in 2008, but the implementing regulations have not been issued. Therefore, a HECM cannot be placed on a cooperative property at present.

Day 366 The day when access to remaining line of credit is allowed at 0.5% initial MIP.

Delinquent Federal Debt Outstanding federal debt is acceptable if the borrower has a payment agreement and is making payments as agreed.

Effective Rate The interest assessed on a HECM loan balance that includes Mortgage Insurance Premium. Composed of index + margin + MIP.

Eligible Non-Borrowing Spouse A spouse, declared at closing, who will be eligible for a deferral period should the borrower die. Refer to most-recent Mortgagee Letters for NBS treatment for loans originated before August 4, 2014.

Expected (Average) Rate HECM credit determinant rate. The Expected Rate is fixed for the life of the loan and is used for any future payment plan change calculations. Currently the Expected Rate is the ten-year Libor swap rate (www.federalreserve.gov/releases/h15/update). It is never used to calculate accrued interest once the loan has closed. Rather, this rate is meant to be a predictor of the rates that could be charged over the life of the loan. The higher the Expected Rate, the less money is available at closing. For the purposes of calculating the Principal Limit, the Principal Limit factor for all HECMs has a floor of 3.0%, regardless of whether the loan has a fixed or adjustable rate. Because of rounding, 3.06% is the lowest rate. Due to rounding and the 3% floor, any Expected Rate of 3.06% or less gives the maximum Principal Limit. Note that 3.06% rounds down to 3.00%, but 3.07% rounds up to 3.125% resulting in less money being available. The HECM has a 120-day rate lock feature such that the swap rate used is the better of the one at application or at closing. The initial credit capacity is much more sensitive to changes in Expected Average Rate than increasing age. For those aged ninety and above, the same Principal Limit factors are used.

FHA Guarantees In the event of lender default, the loan will be assigned to HUD, which will continue to make payments to the borrower based on the original terms of the loan. A HECM is a "non-recourse" loan, which means that a borrower can never owe more than the value of the property at the time the loan is repaid.

FHA Lending Limit In HECM lending, $726,525. Any value in excess is not considered in Principal Limit calculations.

Fixed-Rate HECM An option available to the homeowner. The note rate will not change during the loan life, but the client will not have access to further credit beyond sum drawn at closing. The Expected Rate and Note Rate are identical in fixed-rate loans.

HECM (Home Equity Conversion Mortgage) FHA-insured reverse mortgage with an open-ended term.

HECM for Purchase An option for purchasing a new principal residence using reverse mortgage financing for a portion of the purchase price.

HECM Line of Credit A revolving line of credit that grows in borrowing power as a dependent variable of the Ongoing Principal Limit.

HELOC (Home Equity Line of Credit) This loan requires monthly payments on the interest, or interest and principal, and has a closed term, usually ten years.

Index An index based off the interest rate of a financial instrument or basket of financial instruments. An interest rate index serves as a benchmark used to calculate the interest rate charged on financial products such as mortgages.

Ineligible Non-Borrowing Spouse At application, the mortgagee (Lender) must identify any current non-borrowing spouse and must determine if that person is currently eligible or ineligible for a Deferral Period. This determination is a factual determination and cannot be changed or waived by any election. A non-borrowing spouse who meets the FHA qualifying attributes requirements at application for a Deferral

Period is an Eligible Non-Borrowing Spouse and may not elect to be ineligible. Similarly, a non-borrowing spouse who is ineligible at application because he or she does not satisfy the requirements for a Deferral Period may not elect to be eligible.

Initial Disbursement Level Homeowners may not take more than roughly 60% of the benefit at closing unless they are determined to have mandatory obligations such as a current mortgage, a purchase of a new home, or a property settlement agreement in a divorce. In some cases, a slightly larger amount than 60% is allowed.

Initial Net Principal Limit Remainder of available credit once set-asides (if any) and financed closing costs are deducted from the Original Principal Limit.

Initial Principal Limit Funds available at closing based on age, Expected Rate, and Maximum Claim Amount.

Initial Rate The beginning index + margin at loan's inception. Also known as the Note Rate.

Interest Rate Caps For HECM annually adjusting, 5%. For HECM monthly adjusting, 10%.

Jumbo Reverse Mortgage A proprietary reverse mortgage, which is not FHA insured, that may be used when FHA guidelines are not suitable, or in which a client's property exceeds the FHA lending limit. These loans usually have higher interest rates, lower loan to value ratios, and restrictions requiring full draws, no line of credit growth, and no revolving access to line of credit once paid down. There is increasing interest in Jumbo loans and many of the restrictions such as these have been removed.

LESA (Life-Expectancy Set-Asides) Funds put aside either in full or in part for future tax and insurance payments if the client is deemed by the underwriter to be deficient in either willingness or capacity to meet homeowner obligations. A voluntary LESA is a way to manage a retirement budget to account for the fixed expenses caused by taxes and insurance.

Libor (The London Interbank Offered Rate) The average interest rate estimated by leading banks in London that the average leading bank would be charged if borrowing from other banks. The one-month Libor commonly is used as an index for the monthly adjustable-rate HECM.

Libor Ten-year Swap Rate Currently used to calculate Expected Average Rate in HECM loans.

Life Estate The right to live in the home while one or more others own the right to sell the property and to take full possession when the life-estate holder dies or leaves (the "remainder interest"). A HECM can be done on a property where the borrower has only a life-estate interest, as long as the owners of the remainder interest agree.

Living Trust A legal entity created during a person's lifetime to hold the ownership of money and real property, often for estate planning purposes. Property held in a living trust may be eligible if the beneficiaries are eligible HECM borrowers.

LTV Ratio of loan amount to home value. In a HECM, the LTV is known as the Principal Limit. But unlike a traditional mortgage, the Principal Limit grows at the Effective Rate month after month.

Margin The lender's margin is controlled by the lenders and their investors and may vary from lender to lender and from week to week until loan closing. However, once it is set for a particular loan, it never changes throughout the life of the loan. The margin is constant throughout the life of the mortgage, while the index value is variable. For example, the index might be the one-month Libor, which varies according to market conditions, and the margin might be 2.0%. If that Libor rate were 2% and the margin 2.12%, the interest rate would be 4.12%.

Maximum Claim Amount Appraised value of home, or FHA lending limit, whichever is less.

Maximum Fully Indexed Rate For the Adjustable HECM, the index + margin + maximum periodic adjustments. The rates will vary throughout the life of the loan but will never exceed the maximum.

Modified Tenure Payment Borrower may combine a line of credit with monthly payments for as long as one borrower remains in the home (tenure option).

Modified Term Payment Borrower may combine a line of credit with monthly payments for a fixed number of months (term option).

Negative Amortization A loan with a growing loan balance. Carrying costs are added to loan balance when no payments are made in any given month. In a HECM this would be draws, interest, monthly MIP, and any fees set aside for servicing or other purposes.

Non-Recourse No deficiency judgment may be taken against the borrower or the estate should the loan balance exceed the market value of the property.

Note Rate Index + margin in adjustable HECM loans in any given month.

Ongoing Mortgage Insurance Premium (MIP) Calculated on the current loan balance and added on to the loan balance every month. It is typically an advance from the borrower's available funds. This fee, along with the Upfront Mortgage Insurance Premium, provides insurance through FHA to protect both the borrower and lender should the loan balance exceed the home value. Today the rate is 0.5%. The money becomes part of FHA's mortgage insurance fund. This fund is used to pay claims to lenders if the borrower's loan balance exceeds their home value when the loan is paid off. When the loan balance reaches 98% of the Maximum Claim Amount, the lender may assign the loan to HUD and be paid the full loan balance from the mortgage insurance fund. This protection makes the HECM possible for lenders, who now have minimal risk of loss, regardless of what happens to the borrower's home value.

Ongoing Principal Limit Growing credit capacity during HECM loan life tied to Effective Rate.

Origination Fee Compensates the lender for the activities involved in setting up the loan. Although origination fees in the forward mortgage world are typically 1% or less, the origination fee for HECMs is permitted by FHA to be as much as 2% of the first $200,000 of the Maximum Claim Amount plus 1% of additional home value *but* not more than $6,000 total. Lenders may always charge at least $2,500 on lower-value homes and lenders may offer to waive or reduce origination fees. This fee can be negotiated.

Principal Limit Factor Table of values used by FHA to determine how much the Initial Principal Limit will be based on age and expected rate. Applied to Maximum Claim Amount.

Repair Set-Asides If the property does not meet minimum property standards, the borrower must complete required repairs. If the cost of the repairs is less than 15% of the Maximum Claim Amount, the borrower may complete the work after closing. In these cases, the lender attaches a repair rider to the loan agreement, certifying that the work will be completed as required. A repair set-aside of 150% of the estimated cost of the repairs is established, and this credit is not available for any other purpose until the repairs are complete and approved. Once repairs have been inspected and contractors paid, any remaining amount will convert to available credit.

Seasoning Lenders may only permit the payoff of existing non-HECM liens using HECM proceeds if the liens have been in place longer than twelve months or have resulted in less than $500 cash to the mortgagor, whether at closing or through cumulative draws (e.g., as with a HELOC) prior to the date of the initial HECM loan application.

Service Fee Set-Aside (SFSA) If a servicing fee is charged, the lender sets aside from the borrower's Principal

Limit the present value of the total monthly servicing fees from closing until the borrower would reach age 100, taking into account the growth of the Principal Limit. This reduces the funds available to the borrower at closing, typically by $4,000–6,000. This amount is not debt, so it is *not* added to the loan balance at closing. Instead, it is set aside or held in reserve so that it cannot be spent in other ways. The loan servicer deducts its monthly fee from this credit amount and adds it to the loan balance each month during the life of the loan. Few borrowers live to age 100; therefore, the total amount set aside by the HECM program typically inflates the actual total amount likely to be charged on most HECMs during the life of the loan. If the loan is paid off early, the remaining amount in the SFSA is like the line of credit; it reverts to equity. In other words, the set-aside is money that has not been borrowed. There is no refund of the SFSA because it was never charged to the borrower in the first place. Most new HECM loans do not require a service fee set-aside.

Servicer The entity that administers the loan after closing, maintaining records and issuing statements.

Set-Asides Set-asides are not costs because they do not immediately become part of the loan balance. Instead, they represent money reserved for a future purpose. The amounts will be added to the loan balance only when the funds are drawn.

TALC (Total Annual Loan Cost). An annual percentage cost of a reverse mortgage. Different than APR, which takes into account only the finance charges in a credit transaction, the TALC rate considers all costs. In projecting the total cost of credit, TALC rates are based on different loan periods such as two years, a period equal to the youngest consumer's life expectancy, and a period equal to 1.4 times the youngest consumer's life expectancy. TALC rates are based on assumed annual house appreciation rates of 0%, 4%, and 8%. The projected total cost of credit must reflect all costs and charges to the consumer, including the costs of any annuity that the consumer purchases as part of the reverse mortgage transaction. In general, the longer the borrower remains in the house, the lower the total annual loan cost will be.

Tenure Payment Borrower receives monthly payments from the lender for as long as the home is occupied as the principal residence. Although the loan balance is scheduled to equal the Principal Limit when the youngest borrower reaches age 100, payments continue for as long as the borrower lives in the home as a principal residence, no matter how long that is. In effect, the homeowner has used the home, rather than cash, to create an annuity, but an annuity that is not portable to a new residence. If the lender is late sending the payment, the borrower is owed a late fee.

Term Payment Borrower receives monthly payments from the lender for a period of months selected by the borrower. If the lender is late making the payment, the borrower is owed a late fee.

Time Value of Money The concept that the value of a dollar to be received in future is less than the value of a dollar on hand today. One reason is that money received today can be invested, thus generating more money.

Upfront Mortgage Insurance Premium (MIP) Calculated at 2% on Maximum Claim Amount and added to loan balance, unless paid outside of closing. This fee, along with the Ongoing Mortgage Insurance Premium, provides insurance through FHA to protect both the borrower and lender should the loan balance exceed the home value.

Appendix For Advanced Study

Courtesy of www.toolsforretirementplanning.com

A variety of strategies can be used to fund spending when combining reverse mortgages and portfolio draws. Wagner's paper examines five strategies, such as using the reverse mortgage line of credit first before any portfolio withdrawals, fixed monthly draws for thirty years, or monthly tenure advances guaranteed to continue as long as the homeowner stays in the house. All the strategies improved retirement withdrawals. Benefits of each strategy are examined.

Wagner, Gerald C., "The 6.0 Percent Rule", *Journal of Financial Planning*, 26/12 (2013), 46–54. www.onefpa.org/journal/Pages/The%206.0%20Percent%20Rule.aspx

With only the portfolio to fund spending, sustainable withdrawals were 3.75%. In contrast, with a thirty-year spending horizon and first-year withdrawal of 6.0%, reverse mortgage scheduled advances as a portfolio supplement give "spending success" levels of 88% to 92%. Even with a first-year withdrawal of 6.5%, success levels are still 83% to 86%. This paper provides financial planners with a review of the relative merits of using a reverse mortgage as a retirement spending supplement. After fifteen years, the client's estate value is 10% to 30% higher using the reverse mortgage plus portfolio than relying on the portfolio alone, combining current portfolio, home value, and deducting the reverse mortgage loan balance.

Sacks, Barry H., and Stephen R. Sacks, "Reversing the Conventional Wisdom: Using Home Equity to Supplement Retirement Income", *Journal of Financial Planning*, 25/2 (December 2012), 43–52. www.onefpa.org/journal/Pages/ Reversing the Conventional Wisdom Using Home Equity to Supplement Retirement Income.aspx

This paper examines three strategies for using home equity, in the form of a reverse mortgage credit line, to increase the safe maximum initial rate of retirement income withdrawals.

Peter Neuwirth, Barry H. Sacks, and Stephen R. Sacks, "Integrating Home Equity and Retirement Savings through the Rule of 30", *Journal of Financial Planning*, 30/10 (October 2017), 52–62. www.onefpa.org/journal/ Pages/OCT17-Integrating-Home-Equity-and-Retirement-Savings-through-the-Rule-of-30.aspx

Combining home equity with even modest retirement accounts can improve spending.

Standby Reverse Mortgage: Borrow from then Repay Line of Credit to Augment Portfolio Withdrawals. A standby reverse mortgage is a strategy of borrowing from the HECM line of credit when the portfolio has suffered a significant downturn and repaying it after the portfolio recovers so it is available to help future spending in the future. The team of Salter, Pfeiffer, and Evensky introduced this concept.

Pfeiffer, Shaun, C. Angus Schaal, and John Salter, "HECM Reverse Mortgages: Now or Last Resort?" *Journal of Financial Planning,* 27/5 (2014), 44–51. https://www.onefpa. org/journal/Pages/MAY14-HECM-Reverse-Mortgages-Now-or-Last-Resort.aspx

This study outlines recent changes in the reverse mortgage market and investigates plan survival rates for distribution strategies that establish a Home Equity Conversion Mortgage (HECM) reverse mortgage line of credit at the beginning of retirement and as a last resort. Early establishment of a HECM line of credit in the current low interest rate environment is shown to consistently provide higher thirty-year survival rates than those shown for the last-resort strategies. The early establishment survival advantage for real withdrawal rates at or above 5% is estimated to begin between fifteen and twenty years after loan origination and is shown to be as high as 31% age points, or 85%, greater than the last-resort survival rates.

Pfeiffer, Shaun, John Salter, and Harold Evensky, "Increasing the Sustainable Withdrawal Rate Using the Standby Reverse Mortgage", *Journal of Financial Planning,* 26/12 (2013), 55–62. https://www.onefpa.org/journal/Pages/ December-2013-Increasing-the-Sustainable-Withdrawal-Rate-Using-the-Standby-Reverse-Mortgage.aspx

Sustainable withdrawal rates jumped from 3.15% to 5% and 6% with a standby HECM line of credit. The real key, not directly addressed in the article, is the size of the line of credit in relation to the portfolio. Clients had an important boost in sustainable spending with a line of credit as small as 8%–10% of the portfolio. The authors note, "The findings from this research suggest that the adage of using a reverse mortgage as a last resort could be a huge mistake in a rising interest rate environment where a retiree waits to set up a line of credit in the future."

Pfau, Wade, *Reverse Mortgages: How to Use a Reverse Mortgage to Secure Your Retirement* (2nd edition). Retirement Researcher's Guide Series (2018). Retirement Researcher Media.

Hopkins, Jamie, *Rewirement: Rewiring the Way You Think About Retirement* (2018).

Miscellaneous

Davison, Tom, and Keith Turner, "The Reverse Mortgage: A Strategic Lifetime Income Planning Resource", *The Journal of Retirement*, 3/2 (Fall 2015), 61–79.

https://toolsforretirementplanning.com/2015/11/27/the-reverse-mortgage-a-strategic-lifetime-income-planning-resource.

Giordano, Shelley, "An Alternative Asset to Buffer Sequence-of-Return Risk in Retirement", *The Retirement Management Journal*, 6/1 (2016), 17–26.

Hultquist, Dan, *Understanding Reverse – 2016: Answers to Common Questions – Simplifying the New Reverse Mortgage* (2016). CreateSpace.

Kitces, Michael, "A Fresh Look at the Reverse Mortgage", *The Kitces Report*, (October 2011).

Kitces, Michael, "Evaluating Reverse Mortgage Strategies", *The Kitces Report*, (November 2011).

Kitces, Michael, "Is a Reverse Mortgage Better Than Keeping a Traditional Amortizing Mortgage in Retirement?" *Nerd's Eye View*, (September 18, 2013). www.kitces.com/blog/is-a-reverse-mortgage-better-than-keeping-a-traditional-amortizing-mortgage-in-retirement

Kitces, Michael, "Taking a Fresh Look at Reverse Mortgages in Retirement", AICPA Advanced Personal Financial Planning Conference, January 21, 2014.

Acknowledgments

Thank you to Bruce McPherson of San Diego for his excellent edits to the first edition. Others who helped round out the second edition are Tamara Burden and, most especially, Dr. Barb Stucki. Many people have helped me become the home equity activist that I am today. I am especially grateful for the collaborative work done by the Home Equity Reverse Originator team at Retirement Funding Solutions, a subsidiary of Mutual of Omaha Bank. They are on the front lines battling rampant misconceptions and bias to the point they are often treated with suspicion and disrespect despite the fact that most reverse mortgage loan officers are strongly motivated to improve the lives of homeowners. So many individuals have helped hone our message that it is difficult to name them all. Jim Spicka of Idaho often reminds me to consider the future value of setting up a HECM line of credit early since it will grow in lockstep with interest rates. Perhaps there is no better technician than James Veale, who is generous and responsive with his understanding of HECM intricacies. I thank him and Tom Davison for their patience in explaining the numbers. Thank you to Dan Hultquist who has endless patience with the changing vagaries of HECM underwriting and servicing. Launi Cooper, Mark Schumacher, and Jan Jordan kindly allowed me to practice on their referral partners. Thanks to Colleen Rideout and Steve Thomas of Colorado who have done excellent work making HECM lending accessible to the NAIFA organization. Thank you to Michael Banner for his unrelenting enthusiasm. There is no one in the industry with more inexhaustible energy than Chris Bruser. Thank you to Burgess Kegan for his work in Washington, DC and service on behalf of the greater good. Marshall Gallop of Florida shared the original Excel program that helped me develop the Housing Wealth Optimizer calculator. The ever diligent Dan Casagrande of Santa Cruz is an inspiration to all; with uncommon intelligence and humor, he approaches his work with purpose and joy. Thanks to Richard San Vicente of San Ramon for finding Barry Sacks through LinkedIn and arranging to share a glass of wine in San Francisco. I would like to thank Craig Adamson and Alan Tenney for their help with broker dealer compliance issues. Dan Mooney at HUD answers questions promptly, no matter how cockamamie they may be. Brien Brandenburg has answered my phone calls for twenty years and has been especially helpful with secondary market issues. His fellow North Carolinians Ron Heath and Ken Updegrave are consummate professionals. James Warns, a fellow graduate of the College of William and Mary in Virginia, is my most trusted adviser and is without peer in his meticulous approach to lending. Thanks go to Gregg Smith of One Reverse and Chris Mayer of Longbridge Financial for supporting the Funding Longevity Task Force, Chris Kargacos for his unflagging optimism and work ethic, and Alex Pistone for being the calm, deliberative leader that he is. A special word of thanks again to Chris Mayer for his work at the Columbia Business School Paul Milstein Center for Real Estate, and many of the collaborative projects he shares with Laurie Goodman at the Urban Institute.

Any woman in business needs her own posse. I am grateful to the strong and supportive encouragement given me from admirable women like Shelley Wells, Richelle Hopkins, Barbara Bodner, Sara Cornwall, Heather Johnson, Gina Shackelford, Nicole Walker, Homa Rassouli, Janice Cohen, Debbie Lee, Martha Echols, Ann Marie Harrison, Karen Rayfield, Betty Meredith, Rita Cheng, Sandy Timmermann, Mary Jo Lafaye and, most especially for her extraordinary empathy, Marvis Baehr.

I marvel at the sensitivity shown by such a young man, Jamie Hopkins, who actually seems to enjoy hanging out with the oldsters who populate the reverse mortgage universe. His energy and intelligence have kept us fresh. And a big thank you to David Littell, JD, for recognizing early on what a special person Jamie is.

Thanks to Debbie Lucas at MIT for her passionate advocacy of rational lending principles and Robert C. Merton for carrying the torch around the world.

My friends Torrey Larsen and Joseph Ferraro have been endlessly encouraging. And, finally, I thank Andrew B. Weissman who has understood from the beginning that this book's message is important.

The History Of The Funding Longevity Task Force

In 2012, Torrey Larsen of Synergy 1 Lending asked me to bring together a group of retirement experts for a conversation on the role housing wealth could play in retirement income security. Our first discussion included Barry Sacks, Sandra Timmermann, Rita Cheng, and John Salter. Later we were delighted to welcome Tom Davison to our team—someone whose blog toolsforretirementplanning.com is of continuous help to us. Barry Sacks informed FINRA that its advice on using a reverse mortgage as a last resort was a math error, and that language does not exist any longer on the FINRA website. At a meeting with the Boston College Center for Retirement Research, Wade Pfau heard for the first time about an asset that he had never considered, a reverse mortgage. Intrigued, he tested the research, and not only joined but strengthened our team with his own meticulous scholarship. A bit later, Wade's colleague at the American College of Financial Services, Jamie Hopkins, proposed that we come under the imprimatur of this accredited, non-profit academic institution. Jamie's energy and leadership have led to a significant improvement in media understanding of the reverse mortgage. Although negative, uninformed press still squeaks through, the Task Force considers this improvement in accuracy to be a direct result of our efforts. We are also proud that we have been able to publish three advisories for the industry that address shortcomings on the part of some lenders and servicers.

The Task Force is committed to assuring that financial services professionals abandon the old discredited reverse mortgage strategy of last resort. Curtis Cloke and Betty Meredith have been particularly helpful in identifying the structures within financial planning firms that block a productive discussion with clients in regard to their housing asset. Steve Thomas helps us understand how to position reverse mortgages with those who provide insurance-based financial planning. Peter Neuwirth jumped into the fray and commissioned a study with the University of California at Santa Barbara to examine the FHA Mutual Mortgage Insurance Fund. Barb Stucki lends experience, and an uncommonly organized mind, to the proceedings. And Anna Rappaport sponsors a large and prestigious discussion group with actuaries and other professionals that is an amazingly enlightening read on retiree behaviors. Although not an official member, I would be remiss if I did not mention the help Chris Mayer provides at every challenge.

To have led a group of this stature has been a life-changing event for me. This team of researchers, gerontologists, financial planning practitioners, actuaries, and lenders truly is devoted to helping Boomers understand how powerful their housing wealth could be in planning for a more secure retirement. In 2018, I had the privilege of co-chairing, with Shai Akabas of the Bi-Partisan Policy Center, and Jamie Hopkins, Director of Research at the Carson Group. *The Housing Wealth in Retirement Symposium* was designed to breach silos preventing full integration of all assets in retirement planning.

The Author

For a little background, I earned a BA from the College of William and Mary and an MA from Old Dominion University. I live in Washington, DC and Warrenton, VA. My constant companion is Scout, the Australian Shepherd. I am a member of Women in Housing and Finance, NAIFA, and the FPA. My email address is shelley@longevityview.com. Please write; I'd love to hear from you.

Made in the USA
San Bernardino, CA
02 February 2020